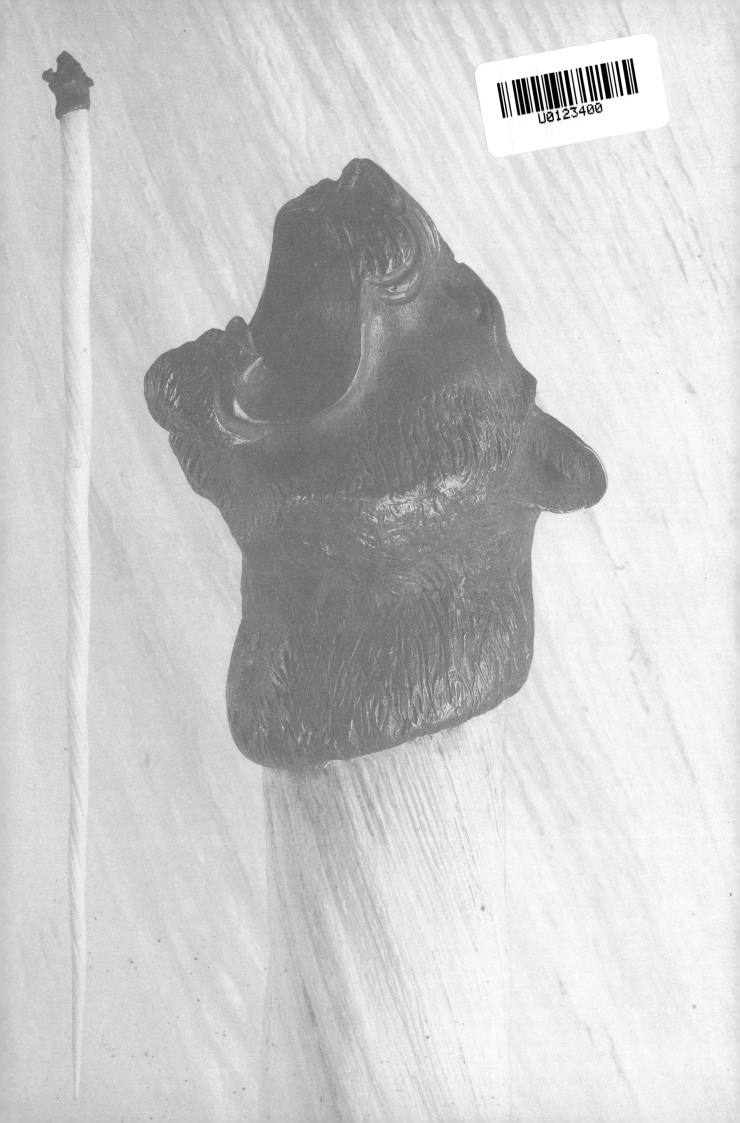

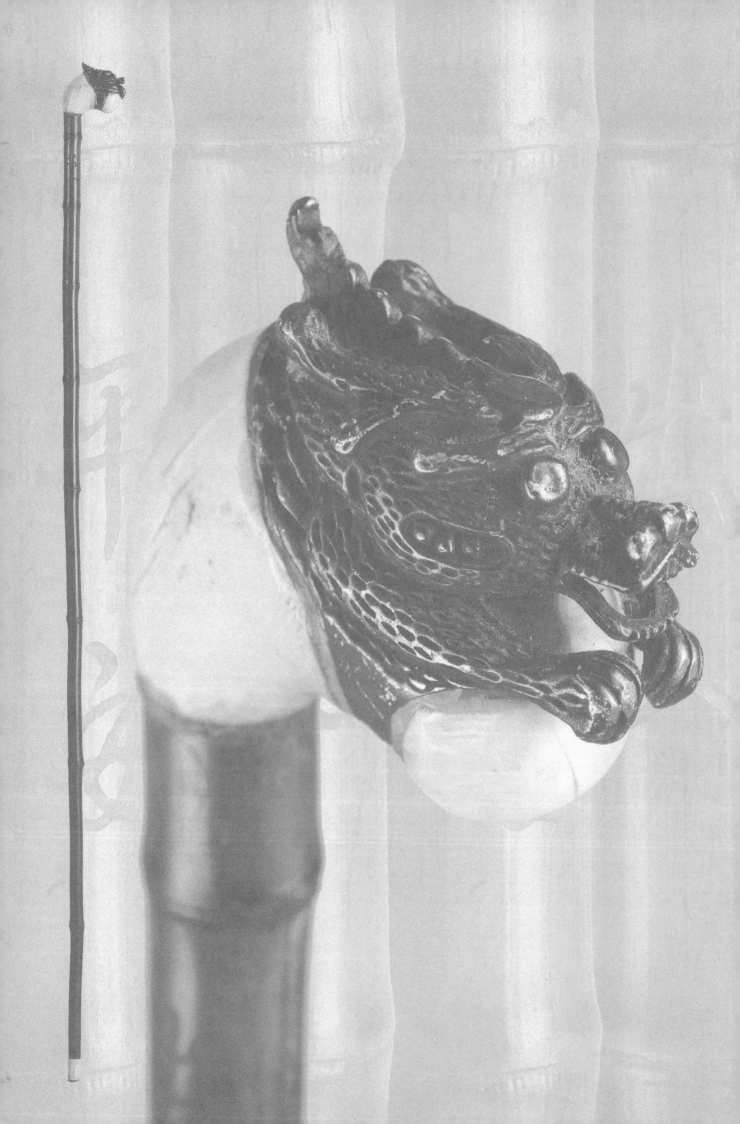

王度杖具珍藏冊

Commanding the Sun and Moon

揮日挑雲

Canes from the Wellington Wang Collection

2008.08.22 ~ 09.21

國立歷史博物館
NATIONAL MUSEUM OF HISTORY

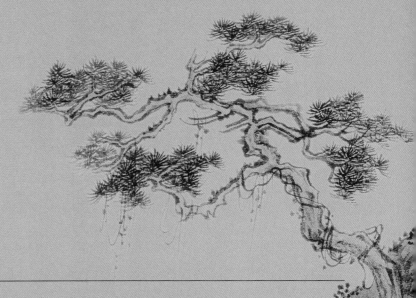

目錄 Contents

館序

　　杖具的工藝發展不僅反應著歷史文化意涵，也是人生命歷程的一環。看似結構簡單，然而杖柄的曲直、杖身的高低、裝飾的表徵，實關係著人體工學。杖具有生活性及實用性的特質，形制爲長且直之木、竹、藤製工具，主要用途爲倚靠支撐、輔助行走，或象徵著豐富文化意涵，如防禦與力量、權力與名望、尊榮與優雅、領導與地位等。

　　杖具最早源自於畜牧所使用之工具，後引申用爲儀式之權杖。在古埃及文明中認爲杖具不僅伴隨人的一生，更可協助靈魂航向來生的旅程。在中國神話故事「夸父追日」裡，夸父死時扔下的杖具，幻化爲彩霞般的桃林；福祿壽三星中的壽星老人，形象爲持杖之白鬚老翁，象徵著延年益壽及親情，更是表達敬老、重視孝道之吉祥符號。

　　歐洲文明中，持杖者常爲君王或權力擁有者；自十九世紀開始，自由與反動的力量伴隨著革命而來，此時中產階級以杖具代表政權，或時尚必備裝束，呈現出個人品味與優雅儀禮；藉著手持細長且裝飾高貴杖頭的杖具，以及行走時不經意流露的神態，透露出一個人最私密的面相。杖具略分爲三部份，杖柄、杖身、杖頭尖；杖具的材質與造型多變，尤以杖柄部份最爲精采，除鑲嵌象牙、犀牛角、珍珠、寶石、金銀、漆器等珍貴材質，亦有賦予杖具不同功能的作法，例如將刀劍置於杖具內，或於杖柄設置羅盤等，杖具雕刻設計則呈現出不同文化的藝術精髓，也開啓了杖具收藏之風氣

　　本展展出收藏家王度先生多年收藏，引介臺灣觀眾對於杖具的了解。展期適逢重陽節，效仿《續後漢書・禮儀志》中，漢明帝贈與長者王杖之美談，今得王度先生贊助，每日限量致贈來館參觀長者精美多功能杖具，藉祝福壽康寧，並期許敬老道德與傳統美意綿延不斷，代代相傳。

國立歷史博物館 館長

黃永川 謹識

Preface

The evolution of the craft of cane-making not only reflects cultural history, but also represents a link to human life. At a quick glance, it appears simple, but in reality, the curvature of the handle, the length of the shaft, and the decorative aspects of the cane reveal insights into human beings. Canes function as an integral aspect of human life. Typically long and straight, they are made of wood, bamboo, and rattan. The main purpose of canes is to offer support, to assist walkers, and to act as symbols of power, strength, authority, fame, glory, grace, leadership, and social status.

In its earliest form, the cane was a tool for herding livestock, and it later became a ceremonial scepter. Ancient Egyptians believed that the cane accompanied a person throughout his/her life and could direct the deceased soul to its next life. In the Chinese fairytale, "Kua Fu Chasing the Sun," (夸父追日) when Kua Fu (夸父) died and his cane fell to the ground, the cane transformed into a peach blossom forest in an array of beautiful colors, like clouds. Among the Three Deities of Happiness, Prosperity, and Longevity, the Deity of Longevity's image is one of an elderly man holding a cane, who embodies long life and familial love. It is, furthermore, an auspicious figure, symbolizing respect for one's elders and filial piety.

Historically, in European civilizations, the person who typically carried a cane was a king or a person of authority. In the nineteenth century, the era of revolutions brought with it the bourgeoisie's ideas of freedom and agitation. The cane became an emblem of social prestige and an element of contemporary, fashionable attire that evoked personal style and was a past of the elegant social etiquette of the time. Holding a long, slender cane with an ornate handle or grip while walking naturally created the aura of a gentleman and revealed a person's personality.

The cane is divided into three parts: the handle, the shaft, and the ferrule/tip, and the cane's material and its shape continues to evolve, particularly the handle, which can be inlaid with ivory, rhinoceros horn, pearls, gems, gold/silver, lacquer wood. In addition, the cane can have several features; for example, a sword might be hidden inside it or the handle might contain a secret compartment for a compass. Because there is such a wide variety of canes, it has become a popular item among collectors. Finally, the cane's engravings and designs reveal the aesthetic essence of different cultures.

This exhibition displays the collection of Wellington Wang, assembled over many years, with the purpose of introducing the cane to Taiwan audiences. In honor of the Double Ninth Festival, which coincides with the exhibition period, the museum, sponsored by Wellington Wang, will present a multi-purpose cane to each elderly visitor, as the Han Emperor Ming Di (漢明帝) presented a scepter to an elder in *The Sequel of the Book on the Later Han: Ceremonial Etiquette* (續後漢書・禮儀志) in the hopes that the tradition of revering one's elders may yet continue.

Director
National Museum of History

序

　　年輕時常看照片，看到老總統手中總拿一支手杖，印象非常深刻；後來在國外，尤其在倫敦等歐洲大城市，常看到歐美人手中常持一根手杖，感覺很權威又很紳士。我想我年紀大一點後，手中也會拿一支手杖，但承老天爺厚愛，到現在還沒有感到需用手杖。

　　在紐約有手杖專賣店，陳列來自世界各地的手杖，有各種不同形狀及各種不同用途，於是我的收藏之心又動，開始收集手杖，但歐美的手杖實在不便宜，回台灣定居後，乃開始收藏中國及日本之手杖，總共收藏了五百件左右。前故宮博物院院長秦孝儀先生晚年也常持手杖，其中一支就是我送他的。

　　手杖的用途大家都知道，但手杖的工藝之美與製造上之巧妙，則非收藏者能知悉了。我收藏的手杖中有以外在造型取勝的，也有以材質取勝的，更有一些是因其暗藏的機關裝置而引人入勝；換言之，手杖本身不僅有其各色各樣的外在之美，亦有其超人意表的無窮內涵。

　　王度一生承蒙老天厚愛，總想回饋社會。對於這麼精美的手杖展一定要有一些正面的社會意義。於是我請求黃館長安排在重陽節時節展出，而我則捐出一千五百支外銷三合一的伸縮拐杖給殘障人士及六十五歲以上的貧苦老人，館長非常支持，就這樣決定了這次的展覽！

　　在此感謝歷史博物館黃館長永川、高副館長玉珍、蘇秘書啟明、展覽組戈主任思明、推廣教育組徐主任天福、郭長江先生、溫玉珍小姐、黃詩雅小姐等，以及撰寫本展專文的黃春秀女士、給予展覽建議的嵇若昕女士、王行恭先生。更特別感謝我的夫人孫素琴，及攝影師于志暉先生與謝承佑先生、陳銘其先生、陳基河先生。我由衷感謝大家。

中華文物保護協會　榮譽理事長

王度　謹識

Acknowledgements

When I was young, I often saw the picture of former President Chiang Kai-shek (蔣中正), and he always held in his hands a cane, creating a lasting impression. Furthermore, during my frequent visits to London, I also saw European and American gentlemen carrying canes in an elegant, authoritative manner. I concluded that when I became older, I, too, would carry a cane, but with heaven's blessings, I have had the need to use one yet.

In New City, there is an antique specialty store that sold canes from all over the world in a variety of shapes and functions. As a result, I wanted to collect cane. However, Western canes were expensive, so I came back to Taiwan and began collecting Eastern canes. In total, I have collected over 500 canes. The former director of the National Palace Museum, Qin Xiaoyi (秦孝儀), also carries a cane, and his canes includes one which I have given him.

Everyone is familiar with the cane; however, its beauty and ingenuity are only understood by the collectors. I have particularly collected canes with unique shapes or materials and canes with secret hidden gadgets. In other words, the cane represents a variety of external aesthetics, but it also possesses infinite possibilities on the inside.

I, Wellington Wang, have been heavenly blessed; thus, I want to give back to society. I have collaborated with the National Museum of History to create this exhibition on canes. Additionally, I have contributed 1,500 canes that will be given to the elderly and disabled visitors. Finally, only with the enthusiastic support of the National Museum of History's director could this exhibit have been created!

I have many people to thank. Above all, many thanks to director Huang Yung-Chuan, vice director Kao Yu-Chen, secretary Su Chi-Ming, Chief Of Exhibition Division Jeff Ge, Chief Of Educational Progress Hsu Tian-Fu, Mr. Kuo Chang-Chiang, Ms. Wen Yu-Chen, Ms. Julie Huang, and Ms. Huang Chun-Hsiu. Also, thanks to Ms. Chi Jo-Hsin and Mr. David Wang for advises. Especially I want to thank my wife Jessie Wang, and the photographer Yu Zhi-Hui. Last but not least, many thanks to Mr. Mickey Chen, Hsieh Chen-Yo, and Chen Ji-Ho. Sincere thanks to you all.

Wellington Tu Wang

杖具賞趣
以「王度珍藏杖具展」爲例

黃春秀

國立歷史博物館典藏組 研究人員

一、「杖」字釋義

天下之大，無奇不有。本館此次杖具的展覽，應也可括爲一奇吧！因爲，在所謂「玩物喪志」一語裡，因溺於玩賞之趣而遭致「喪志」之斥的「物」之中，一向少見包含「杖具」在內。可見就「玩賞」對象來說，杖具之微，竟爾到了「不足道」的地步。但是，天下之間，何物不繫於人情？何物不關連人性？何物不是出自人生活之需求？豈可就認定「小小杖具，何足道哉？」

先來說「杖」這個字。《說文》：「杖，持也。」《集韻》給它的解釋是：「所以扶行。」再如《禮、曲禮上》：「大夫七十而致事，賜之几杖。」師古的解釋則是：「杖，亦倚任之意也。」所以杖是被定義爲：扶行、倚任之杖。其實「杖」在古代中國人生活裡頗爲常見，既是名詞，也是動詞和形容詞。形容詞如：「杖者」、「杖節」，意思是：執杖的老人、堅貞的節操。動詞如：「杖扶」、「杖斃」，意思是：用杖加以扶持、用杖將人擊斃。而名詞的杖最通用的就是手杖、拐杖等，如：「杖履」、「杖鉢」，指杖和鞋、杖和鉢等人們生活中習用之物。

事實上杖之爲物，不只中國人，西方人亦絕對不陌生。眾所周知，希臘悲劇《伊底帕斯王》（Oedipus）中，伊底帕斯所破解的獅身人面怪物Sphinx那個謎：「什麼動物在最初用四條腿走路，然後用兩條腿，最後用三條腿行走？」它所謂「最後用三條腿行走」，便是指：「人」到暮年，垂垂老矣，兩腳無力，必得撐杖始能行走。可見，在古代西方人生活裡，杖非常必要，甚至等於老人的第三條腿。「杖」還有其他含義，譬如國王的「權杖」意指權力的表徵；「杖刑」的杖則指刑具等。不過，本文討論的「杖具」不擬涉及其他含義，就限定在助行器這部分，而其主要義涵若改用白話說法，則爲：「手杖是一種拿在手上的直條物，可以是一種社交地位的象徵，也可以是一種工具。」*

二、杖具的構成、用途與類別

杖具的構成極簡單，一根細直條物，由上而下分杖握、杖身、杖尖三部分。杖握即人手握處，也叫杖頭、杖首或杖柄，舊式的大多呈彎勾狀，以及刻意構想的肖人形、肖物形、幾何形、線條形等；新式的或西方的就比較多外觀類似杖身往上延伸的平直形狀。因「杖握」一語感覺比較硬，下面一概用「杖頭」來稱呼。杖頭這個部分是杖具加工裝飾的主要部位，當然就是杖具賞玩的重點所在。杖身則是杖的主體部位，主要都是圓形長條，偶而亦有方形長條，或樹藤、樹瘤、樹根、節竹，或骨狀長條等，視所用材質而定。杖尖也稱杖嘴或杖尾，是杖身的最下端，即杖身觸地的部分。舊式的杖尖大多連著杖身、杖頭，通體爲一，平實觸地，不一定尖形；新式的或西方的則常出現削成尖形或另外接一塊尖形底的情形。

至於杖具的用途，更比構成簡單明白；但古和今或中和西略有不同。古代的杖具主要是杖者之具，而杖者指耄耋長者，所以是做爲七十歲以上老人助行所用之具；現在人提到杖具，一般的反應卻是視障人士的助行器。再說中西之不同，比較起來，中國人使用杖具大概就是幫助行路。當然，因爲杖具是老人的持物，而古代的中國人普遍推崇「敬老」，認爲是一種基本的禮貌，致使杖具也順帶成爲威望之表徵。譬如家喻戶曉的楊家將故事裡，大家長佘太君出場之時必定手持「御賜龍頭拐」，威望十足。而西方人持杖，早期是老人的第三條腿；但自英國風盛行以後，手杖便常與高禮帽配套，代表紳士的身分了。

最後說杖具的類別。本館此次王度杖具展的展品，先分爲西方式和中國式兩大類。這是從總體表現風格上來分的，即總合了東西方關於杖具此一物，在使用材質或配置性質或裝飾風味等的不同喜好而做的大區分。先從材質說起，西方式杖具傾向二而合一，將不同材質的杖頭和杖身相互接合，或甚至三而合一，杖尖與杖身、杖頭亦分屬不同材質。但杖尖若有不同，大抵即金屬製成，毋庸贅言，故僅說杖身和杖頭。西方式杖身的材質，從數量的多至少依次來說，約略是：木、竹、藤、牙、銅、銀、玳瑁等。木有包金絲的、竹有包金柄的、牙含鯨魚牙和象牙，而銅亦有包編織紋的。杖頭製成的材質則爲：銀、角、牙、金、銅、鐵、木雕、琺瑯、金屬等。角包括羚羊角、牛角、鹿角；牙包括象牙、野豬牙。琳瑯滿目，取材範圍頗

Appreciation of Canes
Using the Canes from the Wellington Wang's Collection as an Example

Huang Chun-Hsiu

Researcher in the Collection and Preservation Department, National Museum of History

I. Explanation of the Word "Cane"- 杖

Nothing is too strange in the world. In the museum's exhibition on canes, anything goes. Canes are not among the "trivial matters" in the saying "People excessively preoccupied with trivial matters will lose their will." Because canes are not included as "trivial matters," they are usually considered insignificant. However, what in this world was not created for the needs of humankind? Thus, the cane cannot be considered insignificant.

First, let us explain the word "cane". In the traditional Chinese dictionary *Shuo Wen* ("Explaining Simple and Analyzing Compound Characters"), the meaning of "cane" is "to hold." While in *Jiyin* ("Collected Rimes"), "cane" means "to assist man in walking." Moreover, in *The Classic of Rites: Summary of the Rules of Propriety Part 2*, when an official reaches the age of seventy, he may propose retirement to the sovereign, and if the sovereign wishes the official to continue working, he will present a gift of several canes to the official. Yan Shi Gu said, "The cane has the meaning of being appointed to office." Therefore, the word "cane" has two definitions: as an aid for walking and as the appointer of office. The word "cane" can be a noun, a verb, and an adjective in the Chinese language. For example, as an adjective, "杖者" means elderly person who carries the cane and "杖節" means having a firm moral integrity. As a verb, "杖扶" means to be supported by a cane and "杖斃" means to beat a person to death with a cane. Finally, as a noun, the word "cane" is used in "手杖" (cane), "拐杖" (crutches), etc; meanwhile, "杖履" refers to a cane and shoes, and "杖鉢" refers to a cane and a monk's alms bowl.

In reality, the cane is not just an object used by the Chinese, and Westerns are also very familiar with it. For instance, in the well-known story of Oedipus Rex, Oedipus explains the Sphinx' riddle: "What walks on four feet in the morning, two in the afternoon and three at night?" The "three at night" part of the riddle means that when man become old and his two legs are incapable of walking on their own, a cane is needed for support. For this story, we can observe the importance of the cane in Western culture as it was essentially man's third leg. The word "cane" has other meanings. For instance, the king's "scepter" represents power and authority and "flogging" refers to the torture instrument. Yet, this article will not discuss the above mentioned meanings of the word "cane," rather it will only use the "to assist in walking" meaning. In plain, vernacular words, a "cane" is a stick, which one holds and can be a status symbol or a type of tool.

II. The Cane's Construction, Applications, and Classifications

The cane's construction is very simple. A thin, straight item, the cane is divided into three parts from top to bottom: handle, shaft, and ferrule/tip. The handle is where the hand grasps the cane. Usually, the olden-style shape of the handle is curved or carved in the shape of a human or an object, a geometrical shape, a linear shape, etc. In the newer or Western styles of canes, the shaft extends into a flat handle. The handle is the main spot where the decoration process occurs, making it the area that receives the most admiration. The shaft is the main part of the cane's body. It is typically a long, cylindrical shape, but sometimes, it is a long, rectangular shape or in the shape of the cane's material, like rattan, burls, roots, bamboo, or bone. The ferrule or tip is the lowest part of the cane, where the shaft touches the ground. In the olden style, the ferrule/tip is connected to the shaft and is flat, leveled with the floor. While in the newer and Western styles, the shaft is sharpened to make the ferrule/tip pointed, occasionally adding an additional sharpened end to the shaft.

The application of cane is different between ancient and contemporary and between East and West. In ancient times, the cane was mainly an aid used by the elderly, seventy and older, to help support them when walking, but nowadays, when people mention canes, most people think of the cane as an aid for the blind. Now let us compare the cane's application in the East and West. Because the cane helps the elderly and because the Chinese have great respect for their elders, the cane became an esteemed object in the East. For example, in the well-known, Chinese story of Yang Jia Jiang, when She Tai Jun, who is the head of the family, appears, he always carries a cane called "*Yu ci long tou guai,*" (御賜龍頭拐) which makes him a prestigious man. However, in early, Western culture, the cane was the third leg of an elderly person, but when British fashions became popular, the cane was often coupled with the top hat to create the identity of a gentleman.

Finally, let us discuss how canes are classified. The canes from the Wellington Wang Collection are divided into Eastern and Western styles. The canes are categorized according to the overall,

不拘。而從杖身和杖頭顯示的如此多樣材質，明確可證西方式杖具傾向於杖頭和杖身的二合一。至於東方式杖身的材質，照樣由多及少依次來說，約略是：木、竹、藤、漆、金屬等。木包含樹根木、樹瘤木，或在直條木上加掛爬藤，又講究是用紫檀木或黃楊木。竹則往往有節凸出。漆大抵為木胎，或漆紅，或漆黑，往往巧思漆成各種圖案。而因東方杖具以選材為首要之務，杖頭多半與杖身同體，若是另外的接合，則材質為：玉、象牙、金、銀等。

材質之外，可再按其配置或性質，分成：實用杖（CA027）、刀劍杖（CA022）、附件杖（CA105）、藝術杖（CA040）等。實用杖即：老人等不良於行者的助行物。刀劍杖即：杖身內藏放了刀或劍，含有助行和刺殺雙重用途的器物。附件杖是：在杖頭巧作安排，設置出容納小酒瓶、藥瓶、指南針、火柴煙盒等小玩意兒的器物，除助行之外，尚附帶著其他的利用性質。而藝術杖則是兼具了助行的實用性和觀賞的藝術性的手杖，杖頭當然是裝飾重點，但若杖頭與杖身通體合一，則杖身的裝飾亦甚可觀。

CA027
銀包柄竹節杖
竹、銀 長89公分、杖柄長14公分 1909年
Cane with silver handle
Silver (handle), bamboo (shaft); Length 89 cm, length of handle 14 cm; 1909

CA022
象牙柄竹杖
象牙、竹 長85公分、杖柄長7公分 20世紀
杖身內藏長劍
Cane with ivory handle
Ivory (handle), bamboo (shaft); Length 85 cm, length of handle 7 cm; 20th century

CA105
指南針與望遠鏡手杖
銀、木 長93公分 20世紀
Cane with hidden telescope and compass
Silver, wood; Length 93 cm; 20th century

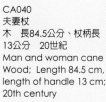

CA040
夫妻杖
木 長84.5公分、杖柄長13公分 20世紀
Man and woman cane
Wood; Length 84.5 cm, length of handle 13 cm; 20th century

三、杖具的裝飾藝術

此次展出的這批杖具共120件。約10件是十九世紀之物，其餘均為二十世紀的製作，年代說來，不算太早。其中有一件「麒麟柄牙竹杖」（CA015），是用大塊象牙做成頭形，其上罩覆銀製的麒麟面，以光滑平直的竹條做杖身，並在杖身兩側刻「出入」、「平安」的字樣，因此行家斷定乃「十九世紀東方外銷至歐洲之杖具」。不用說，麒麟是中國傳說裡的神獸，而中國文字當然是中國事物；可是，極簡極直的杖身，以及杖頭、杖尖的象牙接合，以及麒麟頭面洋溢著的嘉年華面具感，卻是道地的西方情調。換言之，它是採用東方要素，傳達西方風味。所以上面固然提到東西方杖具之間頗有些差異；但單就表現藝術趣味的裝飾主題這個項目來說，東西方之間倒是情境相融，沒有太大的隔閡。不過為了便於理解，接下來還是將展品分東西方兩部分，個別梳理其杖頭杖身的裝飾，俾做進一步討論。

先說東方杖具，杖頭形象最多見的是老翁和猴子，另外則為：鳥、犬、獅、龍、鹿等飛禽走獸，以及花卉等。而杖身的長棍有的外包藤皮或竹皮，企圖模仿蛇的外觀；或寫上詩詞文字；或雕刻花鳥、八仙；或鑲嵌螺鈿；或直接以獸骨做成。換言之，雖是小小的杖頭和細細的杖身，仍盡其可能，視為施展刻、繪、貼、鑲等工藝手法的場域。至於西方杖具，杖頭裡頗多鉤形和球形，其他依次為：犬、龍、獅、鴨、鳳、鷹、鳥、麒麟等飛禽走獸之頭部，龍也有全身的，另又有花草、家徽、人面等。杖身則以素樸的直杖為多，僅有少數通體合一杖身連著杖頭，以藝術加工的琺瑯杖、銀手杖、木雕杖、牙雕杖等，一體成形。但是西方杖具畢竟是杖頭與杖身二者互相接合的為多，而最容易接合的部位必然是靠近杖頭的杖身上端，就好像人以頸部接合在頭與身之間。由於如此便造成了西方杖具一個明顯的特色，即：與杖頭接合的部分，照道理說屬於杖身，是直杖的上部，但它使用的材質或藝術加工，卻和杖頭一致，反而和杖身做明顯的劃分。譬如鳳首杖（CA005）、銅鴨首木杖（CA095）、銅龍首木杖（CA096）、包金柄竹杖（CA024）等。

概括來說，東西方杖具的藝術表現有幾點異同。相異點是：一、東方杖具講究「天然至上」，注重選材，較多是頭、身、尾一貫的一根杖。這是因為中國人崇尚天然，喜愛「因材施用」，往往特選有彎勾的、有凸塊的，以及天生而成拐杖形的木或竹或藤，使手握之處不必另行製作，也使材質之巧勝過人工造作，如仙翁樹瘤杖（CA043）、竹節杖（CA062）、木藤杖（CA054）等等。而西方杖具講究「簡單至上」，舉「象牙首木杖」（CA035）為例。它通體就是一根直杖。杖頭部分質材是象牙，杖身是木，二者接合處包覆著以徽章為主要花紋的銀製寬環。象

outward appearance, including its material, application, and decorative style. To begin with the material of canes, Western style canes usually combine two different materials for the handle and shaft, and sometimes, three separate materials are used for the handle, shaft, and ferrule/tip. Although there is some deviation, most canes have metal ferrules/tips; thus, we will only discuss, here, the cane's handle and shaft. The materials of Western cane's shafts, from most to least widely used, are wood, bamboo, rattan, ivory, copper, silver, tortoise-shell, etc. The woods are inlaid with gold thread, the bamboos are foiled with gold leafing, the ivory comes from narwhal and elephant tusks, and the copper is thread weaved onto a copper shaft. Meanwhile, the materials of Western-style handles are made from silver, animal horn/antler, ivory, gold, copper, iron, woodcarving, enamel, metal, etc. The animal horn/antler includes those from antelopes, cattle, and deer, while the ivory includes elephant and boar tusks. Thus, the materials of Western canes are extremely diverse, and we can note the preference of Westerners to use separate materials for the handle and shaft. Contrastingly, in the East, the material of canes, from most to least widely used, are wood, bamboo, rattan, lacquer, metal, etc. The wood, usually either sandalwood or boxwood, includes those from the tree's roots or burl, and sometimes rattan is wrapped around the wood. In the bamboo, the nodes (where the bamboo segments) protrudes. The lacquered canes are wood ones coated with layers of lacquer, usually red or black, to create different designs and patterns. Because Easterners hold great importance in the selection of materials, Eastern-style canes are typically made from a single material. Occasionally, if another material is included, then it would typically be jade, ivory, gold, silver, etc.

Other than the material, canes can also be categorized through its application, including practical canes (CA027), sword canes (CA022), gadget canes (CA105), aesthetic canes (CA040), etc. Practical canes are used to aid the elderly and disabled when walking. Sword canes contain hidden swords and daggers, giving them a dual-purpose as a walking aid and a weapon. Gadget canes are designed with a secret compartment in the handle to contain objects, such as wine flasks, medicine bottles, compasses, matches, cigarette cases, and other small gadgets, which provide these canes with a secondary purpose in addition to being a walking aid. Finally, aesthetic canes help aid the elderly and disabled, and it also serves as a form of art with the handle as the main decorative object. However, if the design encompasses the entire cane, from handle to tip, then the cane is even more splendid.

III. The Cane and Its Decorative Arts

The exhibition is displaying 120 canes with approximately ten from the nineteenth century and the rest from the twentieth century; thus, from this perspective, the collection is rather modern. Among the collection, the Cane with Kilin-shaped handle (CA015)'s handle is made from ivory with a silver mask of a

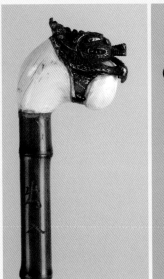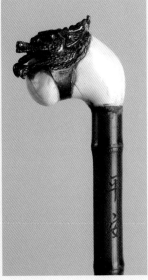

CA015
麒麟柄牙竹杖
象牙、銀、竹身　長88公分　19世紀
Cane with Qilin-shaped handle
Ivory (handle), bamboo (shaft); Length 88 cm; 19th century

kilin's face. Smooth, thin pieces of bamboo are used to pieced together the shaft, and on either side of the shaft is inscribed with "*chu ru*" and "*ping an*" ("wishing you a safe journey"). Experts have concluded that this cane is a nineteenth century export from the East to Europe. The kilin is a Chinese mythical beast, and the words are carved in the Chinese language; however, the simple, straight shaft, the ivory handle and ferrule/tip, and the kilin face that resembles a Carnival mask indicate Western style. Thus, the cane's essence is Eastern, but it also includes a Western flair. Although the difference between Eastern and Western canes was previously mentioned, there is not a significant barrier between these two styles from an artistic perspective. Yet, so as to not confuse readers, we will continue to discuss Eastern and Western-style canes separately.

First, we will begin with Eastern canes. The majority of handles are carved in the shape of monkeys or elderly figures, but they are also carved with birds, dogs, lions, dragons, deer, flowers, plants, etc. Some of the shafts are wrapped in bamboo or rattan skin and made to imitate the appearance of snake skin. Additionally, some shafts are inscribed with poems, carved with flower-and-bird patterns or with the images of the Eight Immortals, inlaid with mother-of-pearl, or made from animal bones. Thus, despite its small size, the craft of cane-making requires several techniques, like carving/engraving, painting, inlaying, etc. In comparison, Western-style handles are typically curved or spherical in shape, but they can also be shaped like the heads of (ranging from most to least common) dogs, dragons, lions, ducks, phoenixes, eagles, birds, and kilins. However, there are also carvings of the entire dragon body, flower and-plants, family crests, human faces, etc. Western canes are normally simple and straight. Although most are not made from a single material, there are a few examples where they are, such as the

CA043
仙翁樹瘤杖
木　長90公分　19世紀
God of Longevity cane
Wood; Length 90 cm; 19th century

CA062
竹節杖
竹　長85.5公分、杖柄長12公分　20世紀
Bamboo cane
Bamboo; Length 85.5 cm, length of handle 12 cm; 20th century

CA054
木藤杖
木藤　長107公分、杖柄長12公分　20世紀
Cane with inscriptions and carvings
Wood; Length 107 cm, length of handle 12 cm; 20th century

至於東西方杖具的相同之處，一是上面舉「麒麟柄牙竹杖」爲例提到的，有些西方杖具是由東方外銷過去，所以出現麒麟、龍、鳳等公認爲東方神獸、神鳥的杖頭物。固然，它是「採用東方要素，傳達西方風味」，歸根究底，西方杖具畢竟還是西方杖具；但單獨就裝飾主題來說，東西方杖具之間確實是有共通點。另一是：東西方地理環境、風土人情、語言文字等皆大大不同，所以東西方的民族性當然亦大大有別。但是，就像上面「杖具的構成、用途與類別」那段落裡所說的，杖具是由「特定的構成、特定的用途、特定的類別」所成之物。而就這點來說，東西方不同的民族性卻毫不妨礙東西方杖具歸屬在相同的，特定構成、特定用途、特定類別裡。

四、結語

時代的腳步愈走愈快，活在二十一世紀的人，享受著前人給予我們的各種便利，享用著從電燈、電話、電影、電視、電腦等串串相連、永不停息的前人的發明創造，特別是科學與科技上的不斷翻新、一日數變。但是，不論科學與科技的變化如何多、如何大，人類的生活亙古常新，人類的生活本質絕對不會變。現在人進入老年，和十餘年前、百餘年前、千餘年前的老人一樣，最後都是用三條腿行走的。所以，杖具賞趣不只是要讓我們觀賞許多人費盡巧思、絞盡腦汁，精心製作出各式各樣令人咋舌贊歎的美妙杖具，也可以讓我們反思內省，人類生活「亙古常新」此一現象所含的生命奧義。

＊註　網路，拐杖和手杖的差異，Yahoo！奇摩知識

牙頭與木身未做任何雕琢，只呈現材質本身的紋理。所以，僅有的裝飾是那圈寬銀環；但簡單之中，卻予人震撼性的美感。相異點二是：東方杖具多用木、竹、漆等輕的質材，根本用途爲扶持老人，或延伸爲賀老人壽的表徵，製成方向亦多一體成形；所以，表現出來的是輕巧的生活趣味，帶有工藝小品的特質。既要易攜帶、易使用，富有實用性，又可從藝術裝飾上的八仙、竹節、龍、鹿等吉祥事物，透露中國人最常見的祈福心意。西方杖具卻在十七、八世紀以後，成爲身分的表徵，甚至讓誇示社會地位的作用大過實用性能的助行。而杖頭杖柄偏向使用重量十足，且昂貴高價的銀、象牙、金、銅等，使西方杖具比同樣出現刀劍杖的東方杖具，另透出一股冷冽森嚴的漠然，含帶著狙擊利器的威嚇性。簡單地說，西方杖具所表現出來的是凝重無情的生活競爭本色，也透露了西方人對生命採取的理性應對姿態。相異點三是：東方杖具的裝飾紋飾，或寫一百個壽字，或鑴刻詩句，或雕刻「竹節鳴蟬」紋（CA060）等，處處顯示欽慕風雅、力求脫俗的文人流風。而西方杖具的主要裝飾是犬、鷹、獅等昂然高舉的頭部，或羚羊角等，隱約透露出動物世界裡狩獵追逐的氛圍，也是對猛勇有力的一種贊頌。

CA035
象牙首木質手杖
象牙、銀、木
長86公分、杖柄長4公分
20世紀
Cane with ivory handle
Ivory (handle), wood (shaft); Length 86 cm, length of handle 4 cm; 20th century

CA060
竹節鳴蟬杖
黃楊木
長94公分、杖柄長12公分
20世紀
Bamboo-shaped cane with a carved cicada
Wood; Length 94 cm, length of handle 12 cm; 20th century

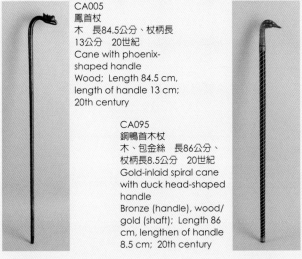

CA005
鳳首杖
木　長84.5公分、杖柄長
13公分　20世紀
Cane with phoenix-
shaped handle
Wood; Length 84.5 cm,
length of handle 13 cm;
20th century

CA095
銅鴨首木杖
木、包金絲　長86公分、
杖柄長8.5公分　20世紀
Gold-inlaid spiral cane
with duck head-shaped
handle
Bronze (handle), wood/
gold (shaft); Length 86
cm, lengthen of handle
8.5 cm; 20th century

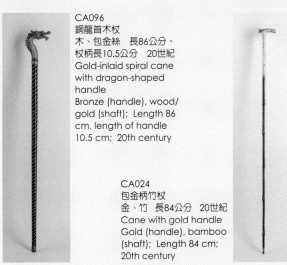

CA096
銅龍首木杖
木、包金絲　長86公分、
杖柄長10.5公分　20世紀
Gold-inlaid spiral cane
with dragon-shaped
handle
Bronze (handle), wood/
gold (shaft); Length 86
cm, length of handle
10.5 cm; 20th century

CA024
包金柄竹杖
金、竹　長84公分　20世紀
Cane with gold handle
Gold (handle), bamboo
(shaft); Length 84 cm;
20th century

canes made from enamel, silver, woodcarvings, ivory, etc. Still, most canes consist of separate handles and shafts. Usually, the handle and shaft connect at the cane's neck, near the top of the shaft, which is characteristic of Western canes. In reality, the cane's neck is at the top of the shaft, but through the cane's material and artistic processing, the neck becomes a part of the handle itself, differencing the neck from the shaft. The following canes illustrate this method: Cane with Phoenix-Shaped Handle (CA005), Gold-Inlaid Spiral Cane with Duck Head-Shaped Handle (CA095), Gold-Inlaid Spiral Cane with Dragon-Shaped Handle (CA096), Cane with Gold Handle (CA024), etc

In summary, there are similarities and differences between the artistic expression in Eastern and Western canes. First, we will discuss the differences. Because Easterners have a great respect for nature, Eastern style canes focus on the selection of materials to create a cane from a single continuous material. Easterners particularly search for woods, bamboos, or rattans that naturally have curves, protruding bumps, or a cane-shape so the craftsmen do not need to create a handle. Thus, the natural quality of the material exceeds the skills of man in Eastern canes, like the God of Longevity cane (CA043), Bamboo cane (CA062), Cane with

inscriptions and carvings (CA054), etc. Westerners prefer a simpler cane. Take the Cane with ivory handle (CA035) as an example. The entire cane is straight with an ivory handle and wooden shaft connected by a silver collar with an emblem. Neither the handle nor the shaft is carved with designs; rather, they retain the natural texture of the materials. Thus, the only decorative aspect of the cane is the silver collar. The simplicity of this cane offers an aesthetic quality to it. The second difference is that in the East, the main purpose of canes is to support the elderly or to act as a symbol of longevity. The figures of the Eight Immortals, bamboo nodes, dragons, deer, and other auspicious symbols carved on canes displays the desire of the Chinese for a long and prosperous life. Meanwhile, after the seventeenth and eighteenth centuries, the cane became a mark of one's identity in the West; thus, the Western cane's primary purpose was as a sign of social status, surpassing its function as a walking aid. The handles on Western canes are typically made from heavier, expensive, high-quality silver, ivory, gold, copper, etc, which causes Western sword canes to emanate a sense of iciness and aggression compared to Eastern sword canes. Therefore, Western canes demonstrate the rationality of Westerners in regards to their life-style. Lastly, the ornamentation on Eastern canes reveals their refined elegance. For example, canes are carved with one hundred "*shou*" ("longevity"), poetic verses, or the appearance of bamboo and a cicada (CA060). Western canes, on the other hand, are decorated with the heads of dogs, eagles, or lions or with an antelope horn; and they capture the atmosphere of the hunt along with the sense of courage and power.

In spite of the difference, there are also similarities between Eastern and Western canes. Like the Cane with Kilin-Shaped Handle, many Eastern canes are carved with mythical beasts, including the kilin, dragon, phoenix. Similarly, many Western canes are also carved with these mythical creatures. Thus, even though the symbolism behind the mythical beasts may be not the same, kilins, dragons, and phoenixes appear on both Eastern and Western canes. Additionally, canes all have a common construction (handle, shaft, ferrule/tip), a common function, and various types of canes for different usages. Although the East and West have different cultures, they do not affect the commonalities between canes.

IV. Conclusion

Living in the twenty-first century, we can enjoy our predecessors' creations, such as electric lamp, telephones, movies, televisions, computers, etc, and these scientific advancements continue to emerge. Yet, no matter how much science and technology change our lives, the basic human necessities will not change. Regardless, if we are an elderly person now or one from ten, a hundred, or thousand years ago, we all need three legs to walk. With so many canes, we can admire and ponder over the meaning of life.

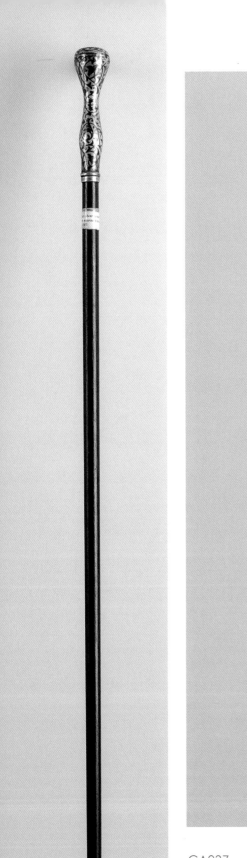

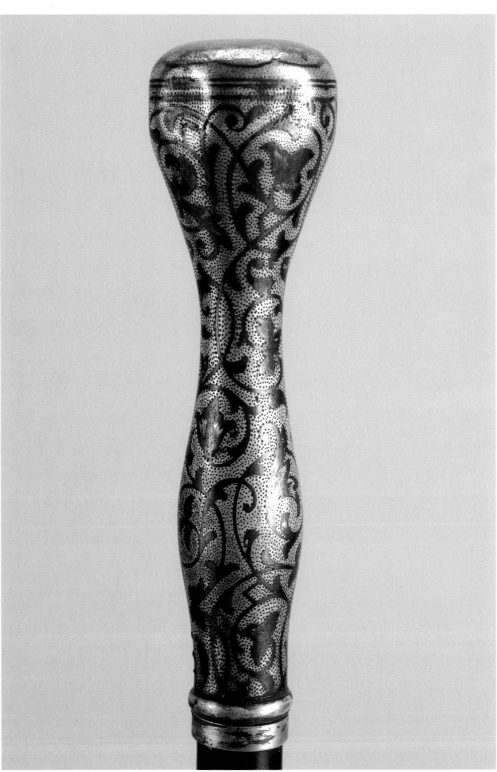

CA037

俄羅斯手杖

金屬、木　長88公分　約1880年

杖首鑲嵌黑色花紋，杖身爲烏木色。

Russian cane with silver and niello handle

Silver and niello (handle), ebony (shaft); length 88 cm; c. 1880

Handle is inlaid with black floral designs, and the shaft is ebony.

Russian silver
handle ebonise
circa 1880

CA090

銀柄扁球首手杖

銀、竹　長103公分、刃長75公分　1832年

銀製之杖柄刻出竹林雅賢，為民間故事中常出現的主題。劍身上刻花紋，杖身內藏西洋劍，杖首頂端刻有「R」與「A」組合之西洋花案字。杖身內部之劍身，倒刻「1832 LaBruna Napoli」（義大利拿坡里）。

Cane with silver, flat, round handle

Silver (handle), bamboo (shaft); length 103 cm, length of blade 75 cm; 1832

The initials "R" and "A" are intertwined on the top of the handle, which also has designs of bamboo forests. The blade of the sword is inscribed with "1832, LaBruna Napoli."

CA033

西班牙家徽紋藤杖

金屬鑲嵌、鐵、藤　長86公分　約1870年

Spanish Malika rattan cane

Metal, iron, rattan;　length 86 cm;　c. 1870

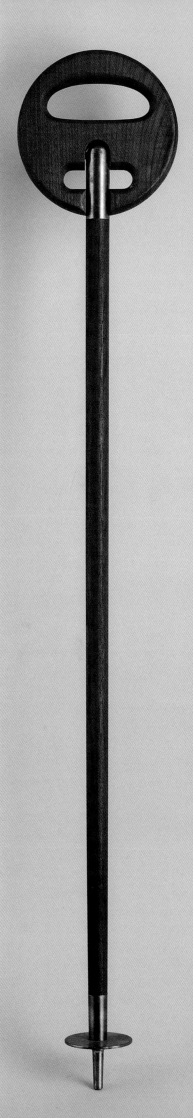

CA110

兩用杖

銅、木　長90公分、杖柄長14.5公分　20世紀

本杖為英國倫敦「荷蘭與荷蘭公司」（Holland & Holland）所製。打高爾夫球運動時，本杖具可下壓上方圓形杖柄，作為休息的椅子。

Dual-purpose cane

Copper (collar), wood; length 90 cm, length of handle 14.5 cm; 20th century

This cane is produced by Holland & Holland. The handle can be used as a seat when resting after playing golf.

CA038

包編織幾何紋手杖

編織表面　長88公分　1888年

印地安人極擅編織，材料來源爲各個地區可入手的植物纖維，本件杖身編織出「DL 1888」之紋樣，應爲印地安原住民所有。

Woven-covered cane

Woven-covered; length 88 cm; 1888

Weaving is a vital part of Native American traditions. The weaving materials come from many areas around North America. The staff is woven with "DL" and "1888," which suggests Native American origin.

CA039

幾何紋竹杖

竹 長103公分 20世紀

刻紋帶有原住民風格，可能爲東南亞之文物。

Cane with carved patterns

Bamboo; length 103 cm; 20th century

Cane is carved with aboriginal patterns that suggest Southeast Asian origin.

CA040

夫妻杖

木　長84.5公分、杖柄長13公分　20世紀

本件具有濃厚非洲風格。木雕爲非洲藝術的大宗，從木雕可發現，其將藝術融入生活的情形。本件木雕在造型表現上，「方」與「圓」、「柔」與「剛」與誇張簡化交錯的形狀安排，顯示非洲藝術傾向抽象造型表現，而頭大身細、上身大下身短小的比例，更顯率眞。

Man and woman cane

Wood; length 84.5 cm, length of handle 13 cm; 20th century

This cane has an African style because the design is abstract and geometrical in shape. Furthermore, the human proportions of the carved figures are large heads with slim bodies.

CA019

羚羊角串果實木杖

羚羊角、非洲果實　長87公分、杖柄長16.5公分　20世紀

杖身由羚羊角與非洲果實拼接而成。

Antelope horn and African fruit cane

Antelope horn, African fruit; length 87 cm, length of handle 16.5 cm; 20th century

The shaft is made from antelope horn and a type of African fruit.

CA031

日本銀箍首木杖

銀、木　長88公分　19世紀

Cane with Japanese Metal handle

Silver (handle), wood (shaft); length 88 cm; Late 19th century

CA122

日本名家竹杖

竹　長164公分、杖柄長4公分　20世紀

杖柄刻有作者「生野德三」之名，生於昭和十七年（西元1926年），爲日本現代工藝名家。收藏之木盒上寫「紫升尺杖」字樣，乃取「紫氣東來雲氣升」之意義，所謂紫氣東來，祥雲朵朵，杖頭上編織的雲紋正象徵著吉祥。

Japanese craftsman's bamboo cane

Bamboo; length 164 cm, length of handle 4 cm; 20th century

The handle is carved with the maker's signature. The collector's box is labeled with "Zi sheng chi zhang" (a lucky symbol), and the handle is also weaved in the shape of a cloud.

CA055

花鳥紋竹杖

竹　長88公分　20世紀

杖身刻滿花鳥紋飾，並有「日本神戶相生橋畔
再奉□命　岩本建春刀」字樣。

Cane carved with flowers and birds

Bamboo; length 88 cm; 20th century

The shaft is carved with floral and bird designs, and
the inscribed words contain the maker's name.

CA056

花鳥紋竹杖

竹　長88.5公分　20世紀

杖身刻滿松與鶴之圖案，並刻「神戶□□
岩本刀」之字樣，應為製作者簽署之名。

Cane carved with pine trees and cranes

Bamboo; length 88.5 cm; 20th century

The entire shaft in carved with pine trees and cranes,
and the inscribed words contains the maker's name.

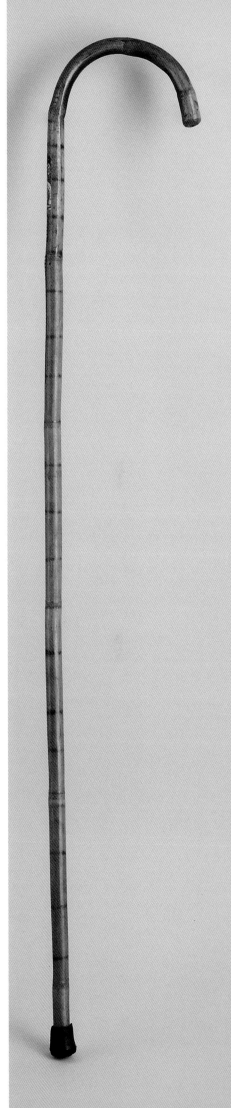

CA102

竹杖

竹　長91公分、杖柄長14.5公分　20世紀

杖柄內側有明顯使用過痕跡，杖身貼上「NEW YORK WORLD'S FAIR, 1939」（紐約世界博覽會）貼紙。

Bamboo cane

Bamboo; length 91 cm, length of handle 14.5 cm; 20th century

The handle has the appearance of being used before, and the label on the cane says "NEW YORK WORLD'S FAIR, 1939".

A Symbol of Power
權力的表徵

杖具象徵著豐富文化意涵，如防禦與力量、權力與名望、尊榮與優雅、領導與地位等。杖具最早源自於畜牧所使用之工具，後引申用為儀式之權杖。在古埃及文明中認為杖具不僅伴隨人的一生，更可協助靈魂航向來生的旅程。聖經上曾提及亞倫（Aaron）與摩西（Moses）的權杖，亞倫代表的宗教上的領袖，而摩西則代表著政治上的領袖，兩者皆手執權杖。摩西帶領希伯來人出埃及，穿越沙漠與分隔紅海是其中最有名的傳奇故事。

西方咸認為人類使用杖具的習慣源自於牧羊人與旅人所使用的必備物品。早在十五世紀，東方的杖具麻六甲海峽被傳至歐洲，並為歐洲紳仕所喜愛。而十七世紀又因傳教的神父使用，將杖具帶往美洲。約十七至十八世紀時，杖具除拐杖助行功能以外，更取代了劍，成為歐洲紳士們裝束必要的一部份。歐洲文明演進中，持杖者常為君王或權力擁有者；自十九世紀開始，自由與反動的力量伴隨著革命而來，此時中產階級以拐杖代表政權，或時尚必備的裝飾配件，以呈現出個人品味與優雅儀禮。

權杖是一種儀式性的工具，是西方貴族或掌權者用來表示權力及地位的象徵物。歐洲皇室持有之權杖，等同於中國古代皇權表徵的玉璽。權杖外表通常不包覆鐵，通常是包覆金、銀材質，或鑲嵌各種寶石，杖首設計常亦有出現家徽紋樣。

曾使俄羅斯擠入歐洲強國之林的伊凡四世（Ivan IV, Иван IV Васильевич, 1530-1584，亦稱伊凡大帝），在沙皇俄國的開國史上佔非常特殊重要的地位，其堅強意志和冷酷無情的性格，以殘忍手段領導，被冠予「恐怖伊凡」與「雷帝」的稱號，據傳伊凡四世盛怒之下，用手杖打死了長子伊凡太子。

本篇參考「杖具的歷史」（History of cane: www.laurencejantzen.com）

The cane has a rich cultural meaning; it represents defense and strength, power and fame, honor and grace, leadership and rank, etc. In its earliest form, the cane was a tool used by shepherds, and it later evolved to become a ceremonial scepter. In ancient Egyptian civilization, the cane was an integral part of the journey to the Underworld, helping to direct the soul along the progression. The Bible depicts both Aaron and Moses with canes; Aaron's is the emblem of sacerdotal leadership, while Moses' is a symbol of royal power. The famous story of Moses leading the Hebrew people out of Egypt and parting the Red Sea mentions his use of a cane.

Westerners consider the cane a necessity for shepherds and travelers. Beginning in the fifteenth century, the Straight of Malacca opened trade between the East and West, and as a result, the cane became a popular item among the Europeans. Later in the seventeenth century, the cane was brought to the Americas by the missionaries. By the seventeenth and eighteenth centuries, the cane was not only a functional tool, but it also became an essential part of European gentlemen's attire as a substitute for the sword. In the evolution of the European civilizations, the holder of the cane was typically a king or a person of authority. However, by the nineteenth century, the era of revolutions brought with it the bourgeoisie's ideas of freedom and agitation. The cane became an emblem of social prestige and an element of contemporary, fashionable attire that evoked personal style and was a part of the elegant social etiquette of the time.

The cane is a symbol of authority, and in the West, it was used by the nobility and people of higher social status. The scepter used by the European imperial families equates to the imperial authority represented by the Imperial Jade Seal of China. Typically, a scepter was not made of iron; rather, it was made from gold or silver, inlaid with precious gems or inscribed with family crests.

In Russian czarist history, the infamous Ivan IV (Ivan the Terrible, иван IV васильевич, 1530-1584) is known for his cruel method of leadership, his stubborn will, and detached personality. He was referred to as Ivan the Terrible and the Tsar of all Russia. It was reported that Ivan IV, in a blaze of passion, killed his eldest son and heir, Ivan Ivanovich, with his cane.

《恐怖伊凡殺子》，列賓（1844-1930），1885年，油彩·畫布，199.5×254公分，收藏地為莫斯科特列恰科夫美術館。
Repin (Iliya Efimovich, 1844-1930), *Ivan the Terrible and His Son Ivan on November 16*, 1885, oil on cnvas, 199.5×254 cm, Tretyakov Gallery, Moscow, Russia.

西方杖具的紋樣

　　西式的杖具大量的引用動物的樣貌作為杖頭裝飾，例如龍、犬獸、老鷹、蛇等，各有不同的代表意義，大多表示使用者本身的威儀及力量。例如獅子向來有萬獸之王之稱，頭部有長鬃，外觀雄壯。龍同時象徵著光明和黑暗、太陽和月亮、陰與陽等，西方的龍形像是擁有鳥翼與蛇或魚的鱗片，並且為守衛珍寶而噴出火焰，相對於東方的龍，在意義上多所不同。而犬獸的意義，不僅作為忠誠品格的象徵，雕飾的樣貌有時亦透露出威猛氣息。

　　老鷹代表著鳥類中的王，亦是是太陽、皇族和神的化身，象徵為天空之神。1782年，美國採取白頭鷹作為國徽的標誌，其後老鷹的符號更代表主權、力量、勝利和榮耀和自由。

　　蛇象徵著生育與生命力，蛇經歷蛻變過程，古時候人類把蛇當做長生不老的健康象徵，更標誌著更新和再生。醫學標誌所使用的「蛇徽」，來自於希臘神話，醫神埃希彼斯（Asclepius）的故事，相傳他經常手持盤繞著靈蛇的神杖，雲遊四方治病救人，後世出於對神醫和靈蛇的崇敬，也為了紀念埃希彼斯，便以「蛇繞拐杖」作為醫學標記。希臘眾神使者赫墨斯（Hermes）所持之手持雙蛇纏繞的儀杖（Caduceus），意指解決了兩條蛇的紛爭，故象徵和平。有的杖頂端有一對天使的翅膀，表示赫墨斯的飛快速度。

Western canes often utilize the shape of an animal's head as the handle, including dragon, beast, eagle, snake, etc, and each animal has a different significance. Yet, most canes represent the users' impressive, dignified manner and strength. For example, the lion as the king of the beasts with its majestic appearance symbolizes power, while the dragon has the dual significance of being a symbol of ying yang- light and dark, sun and moon, positive and negative, etc. The image of the dragon in the West has wings and scales and breathes fire, which is a contrast to the dragons of the East. Finally, the dog is an emblem of loyalty; thus, the dogs carved on canes possess the appearance of power.

As the king of the birds, the eagle is the sun, the incarnation of the emperor and gods, and the symbol of sky deities. In 1782, the United States government adopted the bald-eagle as the national symbol, and henceforth, the eagle came to represent sovereignty, strength, victory, glory, and freedom.

The snake symbolizes birth and vitality, and because of the snake's ability to shed its skin, the ancient regard the snake as the symbol of immorality, health, renewal, and regeneration. The medicinal symbol of the snake and rod originated from the Greek mythology of Asclepius. Story has it that Asclepius travels with a snake curled around a cane to treat patients; thus, to commemorate him, later generations used the Rod of Asclepius as a symbol of healing the sick through medicine. Another Greek god, Hermes carries his caduceus, a short herald's staff entwined by two serpents in the form of a double helix and topped with wings, and it represents peace. The wings on the caduceus indicate Hermes' speed.

世界衛生組織標誌

CA016

犬首象牙杖

象牙、金屬環　長88.5公分、刃長46公分　20世紀

本件杖內藏有短劍。

Cane with dog head-shaped handle

Ivory; length 88.5 cm, length of sword 46 cm; 20th century

The cane is created from eleven pieces of ivory. The shaft contains a hidden dagger.

CA017

圓球首龍紋象牙杖

象牙　長94.5公分、杖柄寬度5公分　19世紀

整根象牙雕刻出九隻龍蟠踞杖身，形制爲西方權杖，雕刻樣式爲中國龍紋。雲紋與龍紋常一併出現，因古人常說龍騰於雲巔。雲與龍代表富貴及尊榮。

Cane with dragon designs and round handle

Ivory; length 94.5 cm, width of handle 5 cm; 19th century

Entire cane is carved with nine dragons. The cane is in the western style but carved with an eastern design. Cloud pattern is always arranged in pairs with dragon pattern. The ancient people said that: "Cloud comes from dragon." Cloud and dragon pattern stands for riches and honors.

33

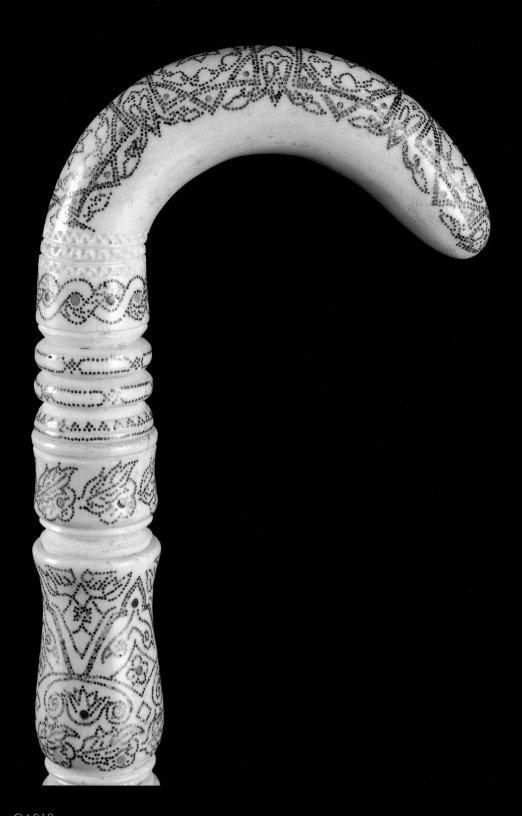

CA018

象牙手杖

象牙　長94公分、杖柄長11.5公分　20世紀

象牙杖由7節組合而成，杖身上所刻花紋似印度風格。

Cane with Indian pattern designs

Ivory; length 94 cm, length of handle 11.5 cm; 20th century

Cane is created from seven pieces of ivory, and the entire cane is carved in an Indian pattern.

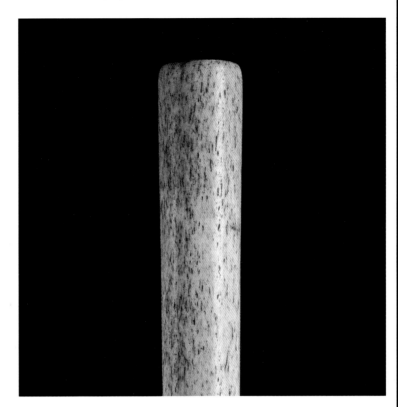

象牙杖

象牙　長87公分　20世紀

Ivory cane

Ivory; length 87 cm; 20th century

CA077

象牙手杖

象牙　長87公分、杖柄長12.5公分　20世紀

Ivory cane

Ivory; length 87 cm, length of handle 12.5 cm; 20th century

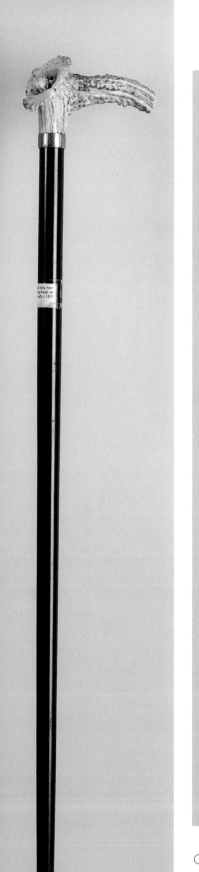

CA012

犬首鹿角柄木杖

鹿角柄、金屬環、木身　長90公分、杖柄長12公分　1870年

將雄鹿角雕刻出狗的頭部，杖身爲烏木色。

Cane with dog head-shaped handle

Stag antler (handle), ebony (shaft); length 90 cm, length of handle 12 cm; 1870

Handle is carved from a stage's antler in the shape of a dog's head, and the shaft is ebony.

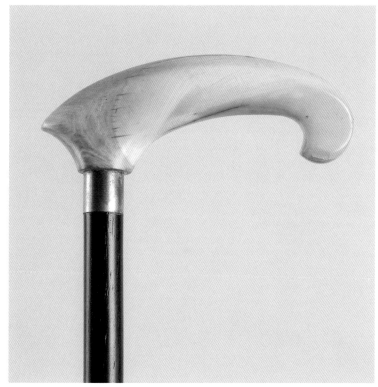

CA023
象牙柄木杖
象牙、木　長87公分、杖柄長12公分　20世紀

Cane with ivory handle
Ivory (handle), wood (shaft); length 87 cm,
length of handle 12 cm; 20th century

CA021
獸牙柄木杖
野豬牙、木　長89公分、杖柄長11.5公分　20世紀

Cane with boar tusk handle
Boar tusk (handle), wood (shaft); length 89 cm,
length of handle 11.5 cm; 20th century

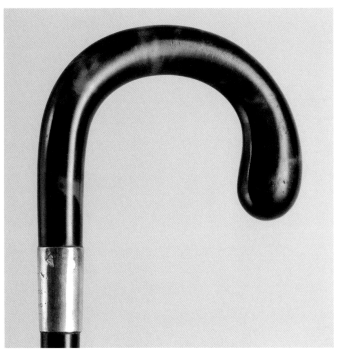

CA099

玳瑁首木杖

玳瑁、金屬環、木　長86.5公分、杖柄長11.5公分　1910年

金屬環處刻「E.H.F. XMAS 1910 AMU」之字樣。

Cane with tortoise shell handle

Tortoise shell (handle), wood (shaft); length 86.5 cm,
length of handle 11.5 cm; 1910

The metal collar of the cane is inscribed with "E.H.F.
XMAS 1910 AMU".

CA020

羚羊角柄木杖

羚羊角、羊蹄、木　長84.5公分　20世紀

Cane with antelope horn handle

Antelope horn (handle), antelope hoof (collar), wood (shaft);
length 84.5 cm; 20th century

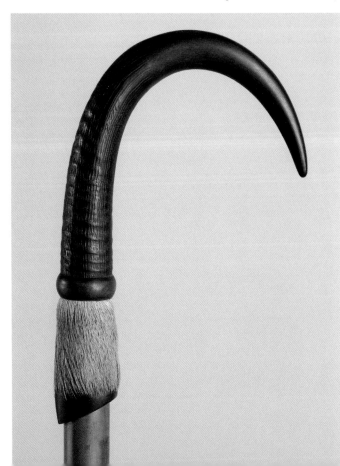

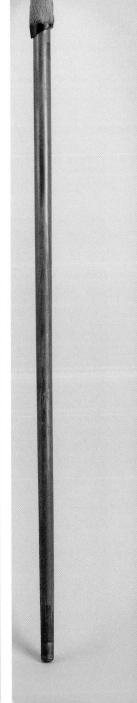

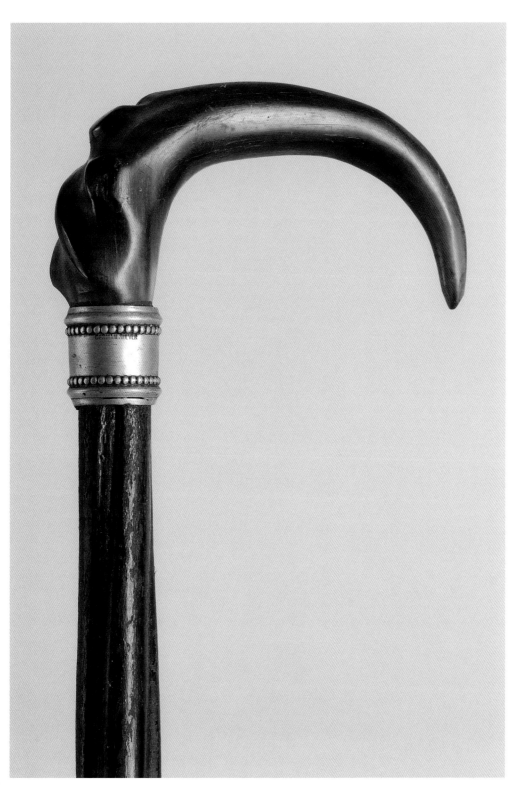

CA109

羖羊角杖

羖羊角、藤　長86公分、杖柄長11公分　20世紀

Cane with antelope horn handle

Antelope horn (handle), rattan (shaft); length860 cm, length of handle 11 cm; 20th century

CA093

獅首獨角鯨牙權杖

金屬、獨角鯨牙　長149公分　20世紀

本杖杖身為珍稀動物獨角鯨（Narwhal, monodon monoceros）之牙，配以金屬獅頭所製成，獨角鯨主要生活在靠近大西洋一側的北極海區域，身長大約四到五公尺長，體重大約九百到一千兩百公斤左右。有螺旋狀長牙，長牙最長約2.7公尺，過去曾經被當作獨角獸的角出售。

Narwhal tusk cane

Metal (handle), Narwhal tusk (shaft); length 149 cm; 20th century

The cane is made from the tusk of a narwhal (monodon monoceros), and the handle is made from metal in the shape of a lion's head. The narwhal lives in the Arctic Ocean, and its length is approximately 4 to 5 meters, while its weight is approximately 900 to 1200 kilograms. The tusk of the narwhal can grow up to 2.7 meters, and previously, the narwhal tusk was used as a substitute for the supposed unicorn horn.

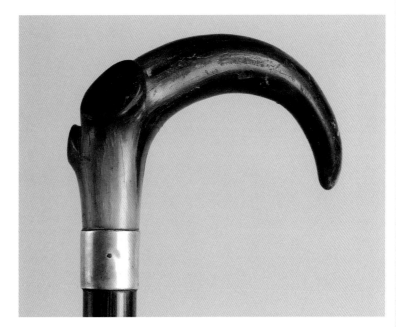

CA116
羚羊角柄手杖
羚羊角、銀環、木　長79公分、杖柄長10.5公分　20世紀

杖身爲木頭打造，仿竹節造型。

Cane with antelope horn handle
Antelope horn (handle), silver (collar), wood (shaft); length 79 cm, length of handle 10.5 cm; 20th century

The shaft is made from wood, but it has the appearance of bamboo.

CA113
海象牙柄木杖
海象牙、木　長89公分、杖柄長11公分、刃長48公分　20世紀

杖身內有短劍，劍身刻有「W.M.B. Johnson (Knife Maker)」之字樣。

Walrus tusk and wood cane
Walrus tusk, wood; length 89 cm, length of handle 11 cm, length of blade 48 cm; 20th century

The shaft contains a hidden dagger, which is inscribed with "W.M.B. Johnson (knife maker)".

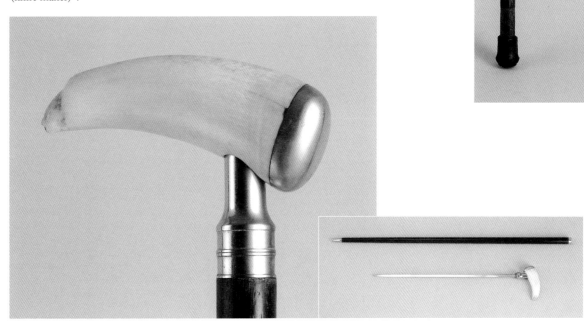

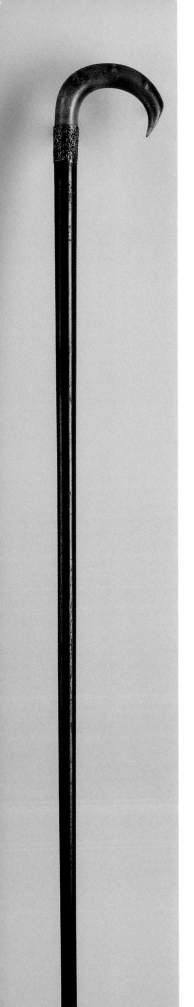

CA108

羚羊角杖

羚羊角　長90公分、杖柄長10公分　20世紀

Cane with antelope horn handle

Antelope horn (handle), wood (shaft); length 90 cm, length of handle 10 cm; 20th century

CA028

琺瑯柄西洋手杖

金屬、木　長92公分、杖柄長14公分　20世紀

Cane with enamel handle

Enamel (handle), wood (shaft); length 92 cm, length of handle 14 cm; 20th century

CA001

人面銀首竹杖

銀首、竹身　長90公分　20世紀

球狀的杖首正面刻為人臉，面部表情嚴肅緊繃，杖頂端有昆蟲攀附。

Cane with silver human face-shaped handle

Silver (handle), wood (shaft); length 90 cm; 20th century

Rounded handle with a human-shaped face carved on the front and an insect on the top.

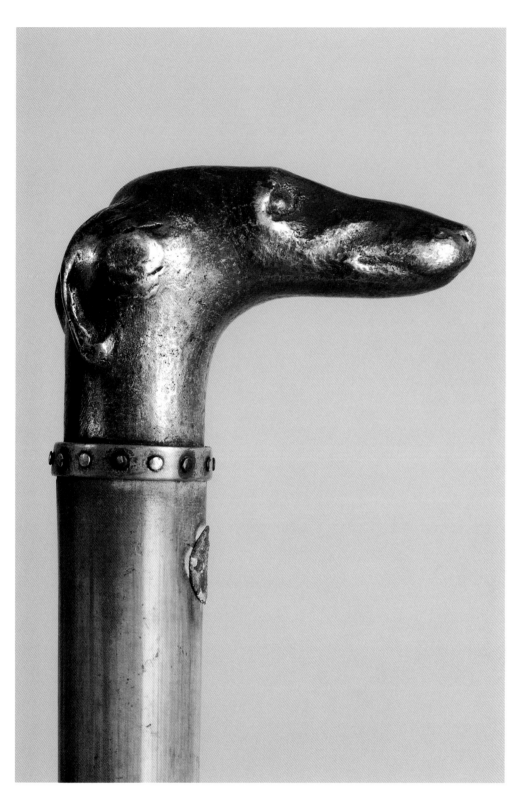

CA010

犬首杖

銀首、竹身　長85公分、杖柄長10公分　20世紀

杖首下方裝飾似品牌之標識。

Cane with silver dog head-shaped handle

Silver (handle), bamboo (shaft); length 85 cm, length of handle 10 cm; 20th century

Under the cane's collar is a metal plaque with the brand's name.

CA002
鴨首木杖
木首、金屬環　長94公分、杖柄長13公分　20世紀

Cane with duck head-shaped handle
Wood; length 94 cm, length of handle 13 cm; 20th century

CA003
鳥首杖
木　長94公分　20世紀

Cane with bird-shaped handle
Wood; length 94 cm; 20th century

鳳首杖

木　長84.5公分、杖柄長13公分　20世紀

杖首部份以陰刻雕繪出鳳凰頭部。

Cane with phoenix-shaped handle

Wood; length 84.5 cm, length of handle 13 cm; 20th century

Handle is carved with a phoenix design.

CA004

龍首杖

木　長102公分　20世紀

全杖一體成形，無拼接痕。

Cane with dragon-shaped handle

Wood; length 102 cm; 20th century

The cane is carved from a single piece of wood.

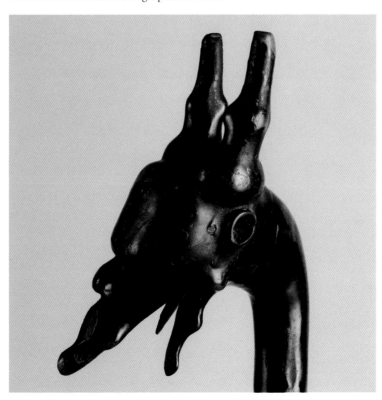

CA009
獅首杖
木、金屬環　長87公分、杖柄長12公分　20世紀

Cane with lion-shaped handle
Wood;　length 87 cm, length of handle 12 cm;　20th century

CA011
鷹首牛角柄木杖
牛角柄、金屬環、木身　長80公分、杖柄長10公分　20世紀

飛行動物中，雄鷹具有迅猛的飛行速度，犀利的眼睛及威猛的形象。本杖雕出雄鷹的樣貌以顯示持有者權力地位。

Cane with eagle-shaped handle
Cattle horn (handle), wood (shaft);　length 80 cm, length of handle 10 cm;　20th century

The cane is carved with the head of an eagle, representing power and status.

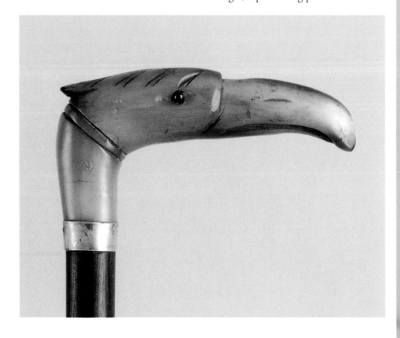

CA025

銀柄西洋杖

銀、木　長88公分、杖柄長12公分　約1890年

銀質曲柄上尚刻有一隻獵犬。

Cane with silver handle

Silver (handle), wood (shaft); length 88 cm, length of handle 12 cm; c. 1890

The silver handle is carved with a hunting dog.

CA014

犬首柄斑竹手杖

象牙、銀環、斑竹身　長77公分、杖柄長7公分　20世紀

杖柄雕刻爲犬首，並依象牙形狀雕出耳朵細部與面部表情，以拼接方式點綴出眼睛部份。杖柄與杖身接縫處飾以銀環，並雕飾出狼的面部。

Cane with dog head-shaped handle

Ivory (handle), bamboo (shaft); length 77 cm, length of handle 7 cm; 20th century

Handle is in the shape of a dog's head, using the shape of the elephant's tusk (ivory) to create the dog's ear and expression. The dog's eyes are additional decorations. Between the handle and the shaft is a silver collar carved with a wolf's face.

CA015

麒麟柄牙竹杖

象牙、銀、竹身　長88公分　19世紀

杖首與杖頭尖皆爲象牙材質，杖身兩側分別刻有「出入」「平安」之字樣，應爲十九世紀東方外銷至歐洲之杖具。

Cane with Kilin-shaped handle

Ivory (handle), bamboo (shaft); length 88 cm; 19th century

Handle and ferrule/tip are ivory. On either side of the shaft is inscribed with "*chu ru*" and "*ping an*" ("wishing you a safe journey"). The cane is a nineteenth century export from the East to Europe.

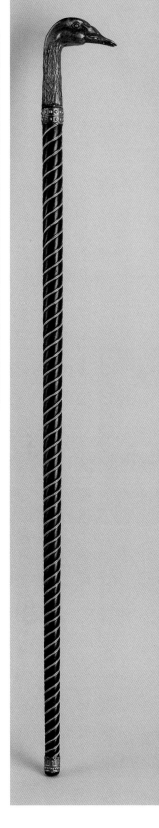

CA095

銅鴨首木杖

木、包金絲　長86公分、杖柄長8.5公分　20世紀

Gold-inlaid spiral cane with duck head-shaped handle

Bronze (handle), wood/gold (shaft);　length 86 cm, length of handle 8.5 cm;
20th century

CA096

銅龍首木杖

木、包金絲　長86公分、杖柄長10.5公分　20世紀

Gold-inlaid spiral cane with dragon-shaped handle

Bronze (handle), wood/gold (shaft);　length 86 cm, length of handle 10.5 cm;
20th century

CA114

竹節手杖

竹、銀環　長91公分、杖柄長12公分　20世紀

杖身上之銀環雕飾著花草紋樣。

Bamboo cane

Bamboo, silver (collar); length 91 cm, length of handle 12 cm; 20th century

The silver collar is etched with a floral design.

CA117

犀角柄直身木杖

犀角、金屬環、木　長89.5公分、杖柄長12公分　20世紀

Wooden cane with rhinoceros horn handle

Rhinoceros horn (handle), metal (collar), wood (shaft); length 89 cm, length of handle 12 cm; 20th century

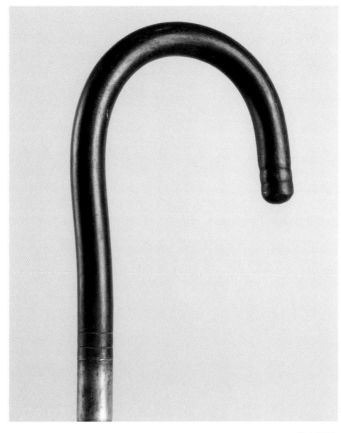

CA026
銅杖

銅　長88公分、杖柄長12公分　20世紀

Bronze cane

Bronze; length 88 cm, length of
handle 12 cm; 20th century

CA027
銀包柄竹節杖

竹、銀　長89公分、杖柄長14公分　1909年

Cane with silver handle

Silver (handle), bamboo (shaft); length 89 cm,
length of handle 14 cm; 1909

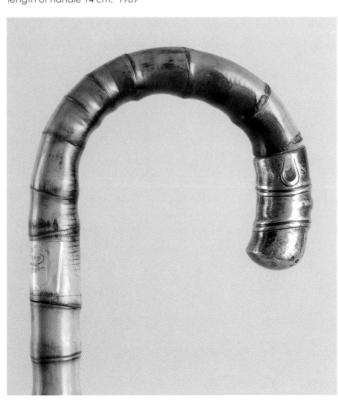

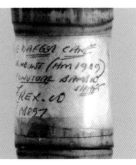

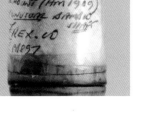

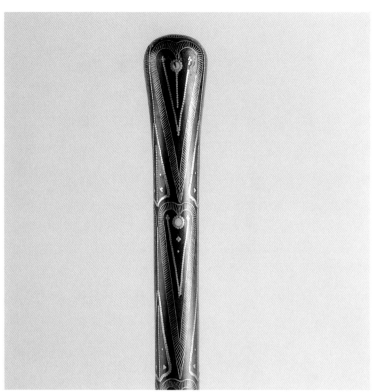

CA041

嵌銀幾何紋直身杖

木、銀絲　長89公分　20世紀

Silver-inlaid cane

Wood, silver thread; length 89 cm; 20th century

CA030

包金首玳瑁杖

金、玳瑁　長90公分　20世紀

Tortoise shell cane with gold handle

Gold (handle), tortoise shell (shaft); length 90 cm; 20th century

CA024
包金柄竹杖
金、竹　長84公分　20世紀

Cane with gold handle
Gold (handle), bamboo (shaft);　length 84 cm;
20th century

CA094
花紋銀柄木杖
銀、木　長94.5公分、杖柄長12公分　20世紀

Cane with silver, floral designs handle
Silver (handle), wood (shaft);　length 94.5 cm, length of handle 12 cm;
20th century

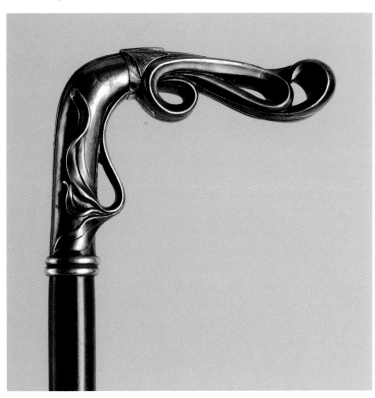

CA032

扁銅球首直身杖

銅首、木身　長109.5公分、杖柄長5公分　20世紀

Cane with flat, round handle

Bronze (handle), wood (shaft); length 109.5 cm, length of handle 5 cm;
20th century

CA034

包銀首直身木杖

象牙、銀、木　長95公分　20世紀

Cane with silver handle

Silver (handle), ivory/wood (shaft); length 95 cm; 20th century

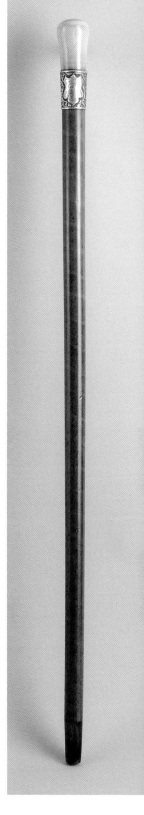

CA035
象牙首木質手杖
象牙、銀、木　長86公分、杖柄長4公分　20世紀

Cane with ivory handle
Ivory (handle), wood (shaft);　length 86 cm, length of handle 4 cm;
20th century

CA036
象牙球首木杖
象牙、琥珀、木　長102公分、杖柄長6公分　20世紀

Tortoise shell cane with ivory, round handle
Ivory (handle), tortoise shell/ rattan (shaft);　length 102 cm,
length of handle 6 cm;　20th century

Significance of Eastern Canes

東方杖具的意義

杖具的意義在東西方文化裡有不同的發展及表現。中國的杖具分為兩種，一種為老年人或因身體需要而使用輔助步行的工具，一為僧人用來乞食的錫杖，亦稱為禪杖。手杖類型，較短的有曲柄，以手握曲柄踏地而行；有長的與眉齊，或高過人頭。材質多為竹木製。老年人使用杖具，最早在《禮記》有「負手曳杖」的記載，杖具又稱為「扶老」，有「扶持而防傾跌」的意思，如陶淵明詩「策扶老以流憩」。可見杖具自古以來是老年人、旅行者的伴具。福祿壽三星中的壽星老人，形象為持杖之白鬚老翁，象徵著長壽與延年益壽，更是表達敬老、重視孝道及親情之吉祥符號。

在中國神話故事《夸父追日》裡，夸父死時扔下的桃木杖，幻化為彩霞般的桃林；《列仙傳》有王烈授赤誠老人九節蒼藤杖，行地如飛的記載；杜甫《望岳》：「安得仙人九節杖，拄到玉女洗頭盆。」另，《茅屋為秋風所破歌》有：「歸來倚杖自歎息」。李白《廬山謠寄盧侍御虛舟》：「手持綠玉杖，朝別黃鶴樓。」，蘇軾所寫《凌虛臺記》中描述太守陳公，杖履逍遙於凌虛臺下，見此地之奇，並派工匠在山前開鑿出一個方池，用挖出的土建造一個高臺。清代詩人袁枚寫下抒懷的《絕命詞》：「賦性生來本野流。手提竹杖過通州。飯籃向曉迎殘月。歌板臨風唱晚秋。兩腳踢翻塵世路。一肩擔盡古今愁。如今不受嗟來食。村犬何須吠不休。」

考據杖具在文學裡的記載，解讀昔日人物的境遇聲聞，或可了解許多關於杖具的故事。許多杖具中的圖像用以呈現民間故事或信仰，例如雕刻「八仙過海」的故事人物；有些杖具將故事內容雕刻滿整個杖身，甚至包含杖柄，例如「壽星杖」以整根木枝雕製而成，工藝師因材施藝，依憑木頭原有的紋理加以紋飾或雕刻。

1. 引自李澤奉等編著（1993），「古器物圖解」，臺北市：萬卷樓圖書，212頁。

The cane's significance has differed in evolution and emergence in Eastern and Western cultures. In Eastern culture, there are two kinds of canes: one is a walking implement for the elderly or disabled and the other is the staff used by Buddhist monks to beg for food, called a monk's cane. Shorter canes have curved handles held by users when walking, but there are also longer canes that are eyebrow-height or even taller than people. Typically, the cane is made of bamboo. The earliest record of the elderly using canes is in The Classic of Rites (禮記), in which Confucius has "his hands crossed behind his back towing a cane." The cane is also called "fu lao" (扶老—"supporting the elderly"), which means "it provides support and prevents falls." It is obvious that the cane has had a significance role since ancient times as a companion for travelers and the elderly. Among the Three Deities of Happiness, Prosperity, and Longevity, the Deity of Longevity's image is one of an elderly man holding a cane, who embodies long life and familial love. Furthermore, it is auspicious figure that symbolizes respect for one's elders and filial piety.

In the Chinese fairytale "Kua Fu Chasing the Sun," (夸父追日) when Kua Fu (夸父) dies and his cane falls to the ground, the cane transforms into a peach blossom forest in an array of beautiful colors like clouds. In Lie Xian Zhuan (列仙傳, Biographies of Immortals), Wang Lie (王烈) gives an honest "old man" a rattan cane that contains nine segments, which allows the old man to walk as if he is flying. Du Fu's poem "My Thatched Hut Wrecked by the Autumn Wind" mentions "I went home then, leaning on my cane, and sighed."

The record of canes in literature reveals the lives of people who lived in the past and can also help people better understand stories about canes. Many canes are carved with images from folk tales; for example, some are carved with characters from "The Eight Immortals Crossing the Sea" story, while others are covered entirely by carving of story, including the handle. For instance, The Deity of Longevity cane is carved from a single branch, and the cane-maker incorporated the original wood's grain into the design.

東方杖具的紋樣

東方的杖具常引用動物樣貌或紋刻經典作為裝飾，代表吉祥美好的意涵，正所謂「圖必有意，意必吉祥」。例如龍首杖、鳳首杖、鳥首杖、壽星杖等，另外有許多依附竹、木、藤等不同材質刻出竹蟬、松鶴或詩詞在杖具表面。

早在中國河南新石器時期遺址，便見「龍」的形象。龍為十二生肖中第五個吉祥動物，民間生活以龍為成語者不少，如「龍鳳呈祥」、「龍蟠虎踞」、「望子成龍」等，皆為祝福國泰民安的吉祥紋飾。本展展出的圓球首龍紋象牙杖，龍身蟠踞整枝象牙杖具，龍姿強調了動態與曲線，並搭配有象徵性的「雲紋」搭配，至為優雅。

道教與民間認為壽星為福祿壽三星之一，又稱南極老人星，是中國神話中的長壽之神。以鹿（象徵祿之意）、蝙蝠（象徵福之意）、鶴、仙桃等作為旁襯，呈現長壽，吉祥之意。壽星老人騎鹿，侍者持仙桃隨之。爵祿封侯的「爵祿」意指爵位與俸祿，以鵲（爵）、蜂（封）、鹿（祿）與猴（侯）來代表，因此猴紋亦常為雕刻藝術中常見題材。

鳥類的紋樣在中國藝術作品中出現得相當早，中國古人選擇鳩鳥作為敬老的象徵，據傳因為鳩鳥是吞食不噎之鳥，意思可能是祝願老年人飲食安康，健康長壽。杖的頂端雕刻有鳩鳥，因此名之為鳩杖。

「倚杖柴門外，臨風聽暮蟬」語出王維《輞川閑居贈裴秀才迪》。中國人以蟬餐風飲露，作為品性高潔的象徵，所以常以蟬表現自己的品行，在《唐詩別裁》裡有「詠蟬者每詠其聲，此獨尊其品格」的記載。

本篇參考成耆仁（2003），「中國紋飾及其象徵意義」，臺北市：國立歷史博物館。

Eastern canes often carved with the images of animals or scenes from folk tales, which are lucky symbols; thus, every image has its meaning, and each image represents good fortune. For example, lucky symbols include dragons, phoenixes, birds, God of Longevity, etc. Additionally, other canes have a combination of auspicious materials along with lucky symbols, such as cicadas carved on bamboo, cranes on pine, or poetic verses on the cane.

During the Neolithic Era in China's Henan Province, the image of the dragon had already appeared. The dragon is the fifth auspicious animal of twelve in the Chinese Zodiac; therefore, there many Chinese proverbs utilize the word "long" meaning "dragon", like "long feng cheng xiang," "long pan hu ju," "wang zi cheng long," etc. In this exhibition, there is an ivory cane with a spherical handle carved entirely with nine dragons, and it emphasizes the dragon's flowing and curved movements. The cane matches the dragons with patterns of clouds, creating an elegant design.

In Taoism and folk religions, the Shou star is one of the three stars, called Fu, Lu, Shou (which represent "Good fortune, Prosperity, Longevity"). He is also referred to as the "star of the South Pole" and is the mythical Chinese God of Longevity. The God of Longevity is often paired with deer (symbolizing prosperity), bats (symbolizing good fortune), or cranes and peaches of immortality (symbolizing longevity). For instance, the God of Longevity can ride on a deer with the god's attendant holds peaches of immortality. Other common images include magpies, bees, deer, and monkeys.

The image of birds also appeared early in Chinese art history. The ancient Chinese chose the dove to symbolize respect for one's elders. According to Chinese folk tales, the dove bird does not choke when swallowing; thus, its image wishes the elders good health and longevity. If the cane's handle is carved with a dove, then it is called a "dove cane."

To quote Wang Wei' "A Message from My Lodge at Wangchuan to Pei Di," "By my thatch door, leaning on my staff, I listen to cicadas in the evening wind." The Chinese use the cicada as a symbol of noble morals and purity. Finally, in the selection of Tang poems, there is a saying, "he who respects the song of cicadas possesses an honorable moral character."

CA042

鳥形柄蛇身手杖

木　長92公分、杖柄長20公分　20世紀

杖首前後雕刻兩人，杖身下方雕飾蛇，以纏繞之姿態出現，並另刻有青蛙，應象徵生命力。

Cane carved with bird, humans, and snake

Wood; length 92 cm, length of handle 20 cm; 20th century

On either side of shaft's upper half is two carved figures, and upon their heads is a bird, which represents longevity. The bottom half of the shaft is carved with a snake and frogs, which symbolize fertility.

CA043

仙翁樹瘤杖

木　長90公分　19世紀

God of Longevity cane

Wood;　length 90 cm;　19th century

CA044

翁首樹瘤杖

木、塗漆　長115公分　20世紀

本杖身塗黑紅漆，杖首刻老翁首，杖身依樹瘤加工刻爲
獅頭。

God of Longevity cane

Red lacquer wood; length 115 cm; 20th century

The shaft is painted with black and red lacquer. The handle is
carved with the head of an elderly figure, and the shaft uses the
original shape of the wood to carve the lion's head.

CA046

翁首詩文竹杖

竹　長96公分　20世紀

杖身刻有「蒼蒼竹林寺　杳杳鐘聲晚　荷笠帶斜陽　青山獨歸遠　龍子題並刻」
字樣。送靈澈　劉長卿

Cane with inscription and aged man-shaped handle

Bamboo; length 96 cm; 20th century

The cane is inscribed with a poem from The Three Hundred Tang Poems.

CA045
翁首八仙杖
木、塗漆　長124公分　20世紀

杖身依樹瘤形，巧雕八仙。

The Eight Immortals cane
Lacquer wood; length 124 cm; 20th century

The cane uses the wood's original abnormal growths to carve the figures of The Eight Immoratals.

CA121
漆雕人物藤杖
木　長184公分　20世紀

Red lacquer cane topped with female deity carving
Rattan; length 184 cm; 20th century

CA048

獅首杖

木　長98公分、杖柄長10公分　20世紀

本杖為樹枝整枝加工，杖頭為中式獅子

Cane with lion-shaped handle

Wood; length 98 cm, length of handle 10 cm; 20th century

Cane carved from a branch with a lion's head on the handle.

CA050

猴首木杖

木　長119公分　20世紀

"Monkey drinking from gourd" cane

Wood; length 119 cm; 20th century

CA053

猴首蛇身杖

木　長100公分、杖柄長12公分　20世紀

杖身塗紅漆，並刻有「金猴獻壽、靈蛇添福
丁卯王能芳刻」之字樣。

Monkey and snake cane

Wood; length 100 cm, length of handle 12 cm;
20th century

The shaft is painted with red lacquer and is
inscribed with words.

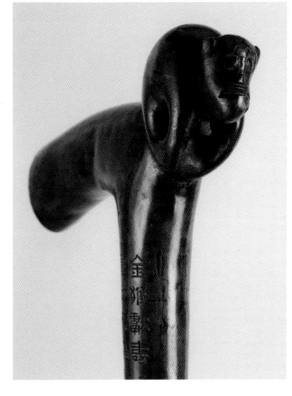

CA049

松下封侯杖

黃揚木樹根　長122公分　20世紀

杖身刻有松樹與猴子，松樹因四季長青的樣貌，因此象徵著長壽不老之
意。本杖所刻之主題爲「松下封侯（猴）」之吉祥語。

"Monkeys playing under pine tree" cane

Wood; length 122 cm; 20th century

The shaft is carved with pine trees and monkeys. Pine trees are evergreens, so
they represent longevity.

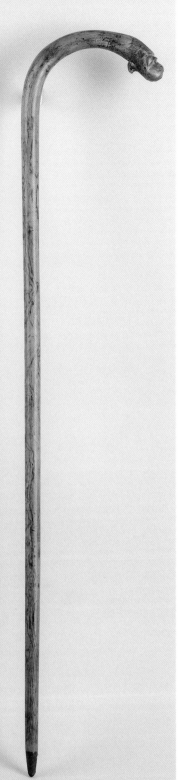

CA052

犬首木杖

木　長87公分、杖柄長18公分　20世紀

杖身之字樣爲銀質鑲嵌。

Cane with dog head-shaped handle

Wood; length 87 cm, length of handle 18 cm; 20th century

The cane is carved from an entire piece of wood, and the shaft uses inlays to create words.

CA058

萬事如意杖

樹藤　長114公分　20世紀

杖身巧刻攀猴，並刻有「萬事如意」字樣。

"Wan shi ru yi" cane

Rattan; length 114 cm; 20th century

The shaft is carved with two monkeys and inscribed with "Wan shi ru yi."

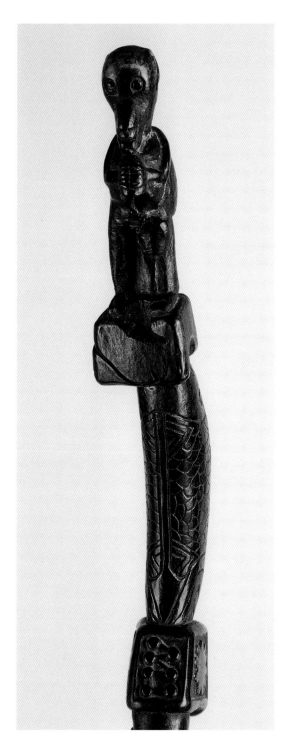

CA047

獸首人形木杖

木　長120公分　19世紀

上方刻有「大膽先鋒、小心後隊」的字樣。柄刻有北斗七星、鯉魚、八卦、星星、花紋，雕刻中夾雜文字與道教符號，中間寫下「龍祥獻瑞、黃鶯喚友」字樣。

並以寫下下列詩文：北斗七星益壽年　齊明日月照光前　文王八卦迎祥瑞　掃去天災海角逐　龍祥鳳舞鯉朝天　有心聖者保平安　鶴在蒼松鹿宴山　喚友黃鶯龜獻瑞　杖然奇異曲彎弓　好笑如同果老翁　履險如夷跨慷慨　當車安步險威風　甲午西山題讚

Eight Trigrams cane

Wood; length 120 cm; 19th century

The cane is inscribed with poetic verses and Taoist symbols, and the handle is carved with designs of the big dipper, carps, trigrams, stars, and flowers.

CA060

竹節鳴蟬杖

黃楊木　長94公分、杖柄長12公分　20世紀

Bamboo-shaped cane with a carved cicada

Wood;　length 94 cm, length of handle 12 cm;
20th century

CA100

竹節鳴蟬杖

黃楊木　長80.5公分、杖柄長11公分　20世紀

杖身由黃楊木製成，雕刻以竹節樣貌，並雕以蟬，作工高雅。

Wood cane carved with cicada

Boxwood;　length 80.5 cm, length of handle 11 cm;　20th century

The shaft is made from boxwood but it has the appearance of bamboo,
and there is also a carving of a cicada.

CA119

牙柄竹身杖

象牙、竹　長83公分　19世紀

杖首與杖底部皆爲象牙，上刻「伯風雅存」，杖首與杖
身皆雕成竹子樣貌。竹身刻有「福如東海　壽比南山
山石道人刻於巳卯　仲秋」字樣。

Bamboo cane with ivory handle

Ivory (handle), bamboo (shaft); length 83 cm; 19th century

Both the handle and the ferrule/tip is made of ivory, and the
handle is inscribed with "bo feng ya cun". The bamboo shaft
is inscribed with well wishing for a long, prosperous life.

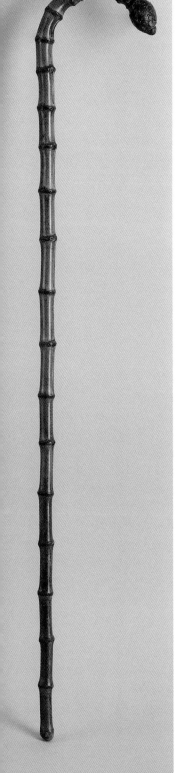

CA120

竹節手杖

竹　長88公分、杖柄長14公分　20世紀

Bamboo cane

Bamboo; length 88 cm, length of handle 14 cm; 20th century

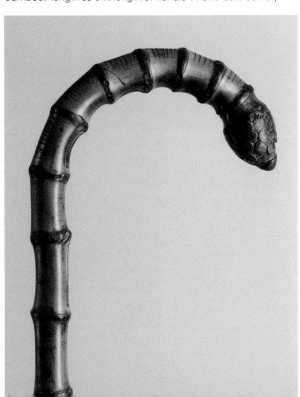

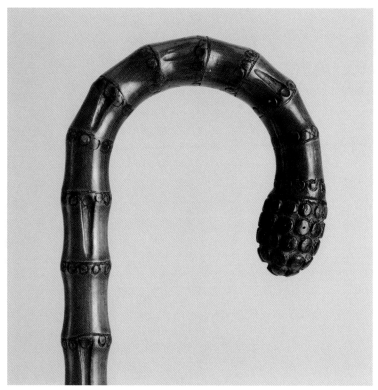

CA062

竹節手杖

竹　長85.5公分、杖柄長12公分　20世紀

Bamboo cane

Bamboo; length 85.5 cm, length of handle 12 cm;
20th century

CA063

竹節手杖

竹　長86公分、杖柄長14.5公分　20世紀

Bamboo cane

Bamboo; length 86 cm, length of handle 14.5 cm;
20th century

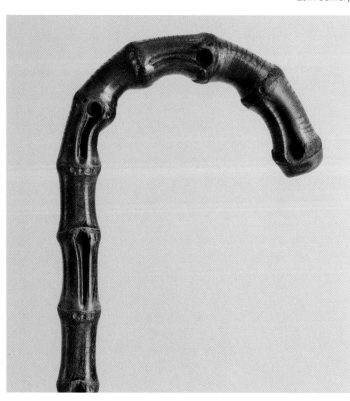

CA059

嵌銀絲百壽杖

木、銀鑲嵌　長87公分、杖柄長11公分　20世紀

紫檀木鑲嵌銀絲，杖身刻有一百個壽字。鑲嵌和漆的工藝巧妙的融為一體，充分的展現了清秀古樸、富貴典雅的藝術風格。

Cane inlaid with one hundred "shou"

Wood with silver inlay; length 87 cm, length of handle 11 cm; 20th century

The red sandalwood cane is inlaid with silver thread to create one hundred "shou" (longevity) into an elegant style.

CA115

嵌銀絲百壽杖

木　長90公分、杖柄長10.5公分　20世紀

Cane inlaid with one hundred "shou"

Wood with silver inlay; length 90 cm, length of handle 10.5 cm; 20th century

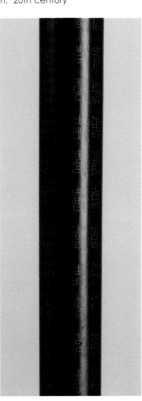

CA070

金首文人杖

金、木　長85公分　19世紀

此件雕工精細，杖身上並雕有竹林及經典故事「堯舜禪讓」、「武吉與姜太公」。

杖具上方之字樣倒刻著「鉤月挑雲　敦溪仁兄賞玩　弟嚴步　敬贈」，下方刻「半耕半讀」字樣。

舜，相傳為中國歷史上的先賢，以受堯的「禪讓」而稱王於天下，當時，國號為「虞」，故稱「虞舜」。由於虞舜執政時，天下太平，風調雨順，舜待繼母以孝，待弟以仁，儒家視為理想人物，是仁孝的典範。

武吉本是樵夫，與姜太公相遇於磻溪，其後發生一連串故事，後來武吉受文王封之為武德將軍。

Cane with carvings and gold handle

Gold (handle), wood (shaft);　length 85 cm;　19th century

The shaft is carved with the design of a bamboo forest and the images from "The Abdication Story of Yao and Shun" and "The Story of Grand Duke Jiang Goes Fishing".

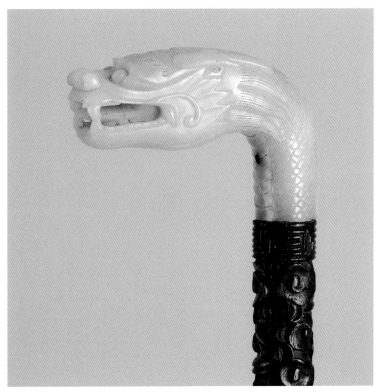

CA072
玉龍首雲紋手杖
玉、紫檀木　長92公分、杖柄長8公分　20世紀

Cane with jade dragon-shaped handle
Jade (handle), wood (shaft); length 92 cm, length of handle 8 cm; 20th century

CA124
玉手杖
墨玉　長84公分、杖柄長6公分　約18世紀

杖頭刻「乾隆年製」字樣。

Jade cane with patterns of lucky symbols
Black jade; length 84 cm, length of handle 6 cm; 18th century

The top of the handle is inscribed with "Qian long nian zhi" (Made during the reign of Qianlong Emperor).

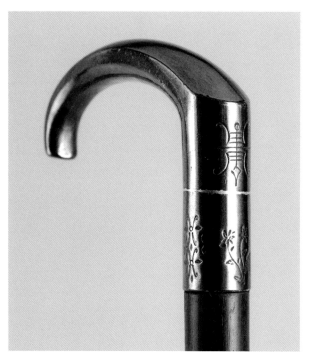

CA080

銀柄壽杖

金屬、紫檀木　長88公分、杖柄長9公分　20世紀

Cane with carvings and silver handle

Silver (handle), wood (shaft); length 88 cm,
length of handle 9 cm; 20th century

CA071

玉首蛇皮杖

蛇皮、竹　長62公分　約1940年

杖身貼覆「蛇皮捆工　日本蛇族研究所　台北市本町一丁目二三番地」字樣之貼
紙。依據蛇皮紋樣，應爲青竹絲。台灣在戰後許多日本制度被廢除，「丁目」源自
於日文，其後「丁目」被改成「段」。

Bamboo cane wrapped in snake skin with jade handle

Jade (handle), snake skin/bamboo (shaft); length 62 cm; Japanese colonial period (1895-1945)

The shaft label says that the skin that wraps the cane is from a Taiwan bamboo viper. The cane
was made during the Japanese colonial period in Taiwan.

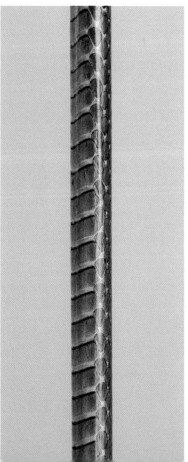

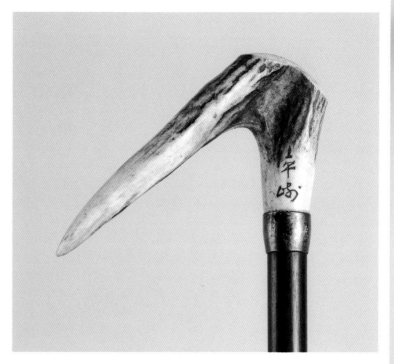

CA078
鹿角柄木杖
鹿角、金屬環、木　長88公分、杖柄長10公分　20世紀
鹿角上刻有「平安」兩字。

Cane with stag horn handle
Stag horn (handle), wood (shaft);　length 88 cm, length of handle 10 cm;　20th century

The words "ping an" (safe and sound) is carved on the stag horn handle.

CA079
鳥首文人杖
象牙、木　長83.5公分、杖柄長5公分　20世紀

Cane with bird head-shaped handle
Ivory (handle), wood (shaft);　length 83.5 cm, length of handle 5 cm;　20th century

CA075

獸足骨杖

獸足、木　長95公分　20世紀

杖身刻有「壽如金石」四字。

Crane bone cane

Crane bone, wood; length 95 cm; 20th century

The shaft is inscribed with the words, "shou ru jin shi" (longevity).

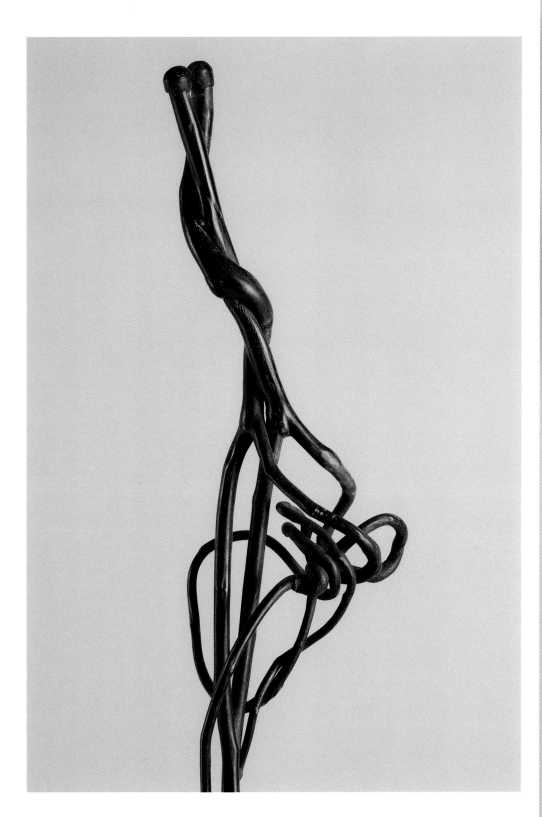

CA111

藤枝手杖

藤　長104公分　19世紀

Rattan cane

Rattan; length 104 cm; 19th century

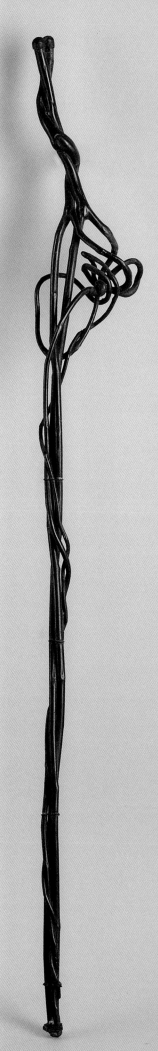

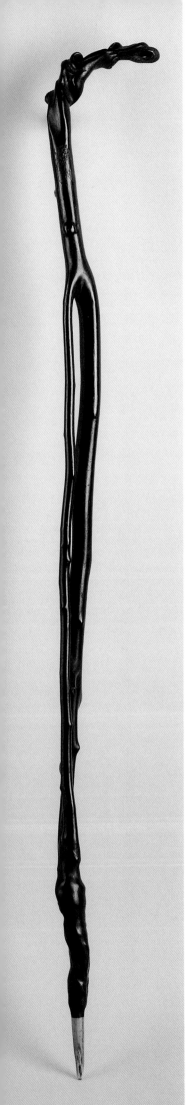

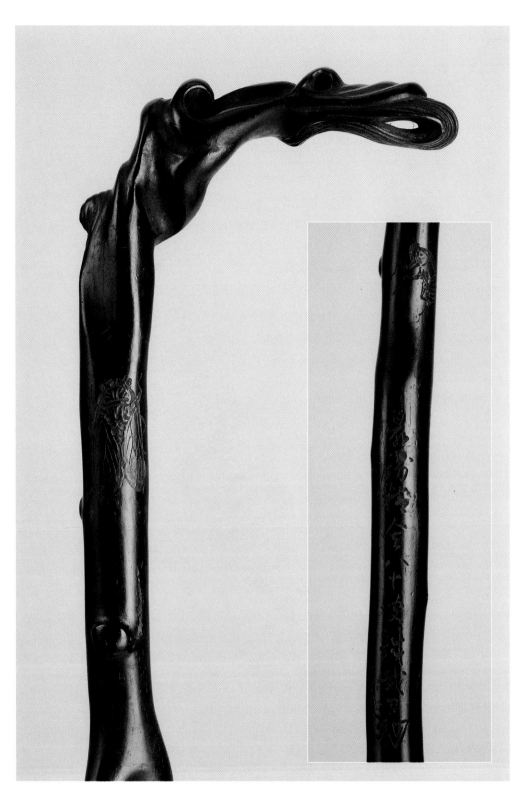

CA054

木藤杖

木藤　長107公分、杖柄長12公分　20世紀

杖由藤木構成，杖身刻文字與蟬的紋樣。

Cane with inscriptions and carvings

Wood; length 107 cm, length of handle 12 cm; 20th century

The cane is made from wood, and the shaft is inscribed with words and includes a cicada carving.

CA107

四方直身杖

象牙、黑漆木胎、獸角　長92公分　20世紀

Cane with ivory, squared handle

Ivory (handle), ebony (shaft), beast horn (ferrule/tip);　length 92 cm;　20th century

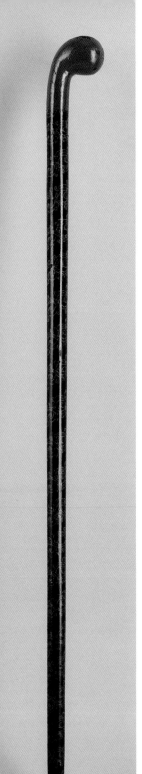

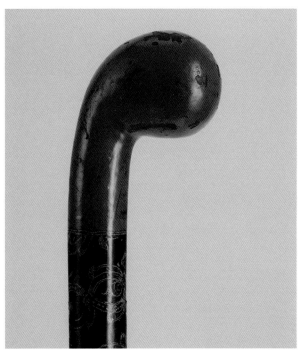

CA073
漆杖
漆身木胎　長92公分、杖柄長6公分　20世紀

杖身佈滿紅、黑紋飾，紅色紋飾之花紋纏繞整枝而不斷，極具特色。

Cane with red lacquer handle
Wood; length 92 cm, length of handle 6 cm; 20th century

The cane is painted with red and black lacquer, and the red-lacquer design is continuous.

CA101
漆杖
黑漆木胎　長92公分、杖柄長11.5公分　20世紀

Red-on-black lacquer cane
Wood; length 92 cm, length of handle 11.5 cm; 20th century

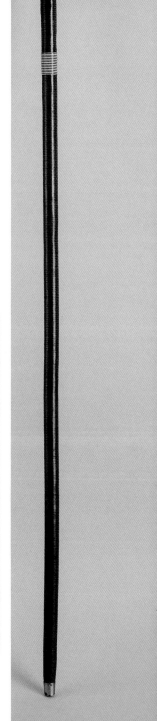

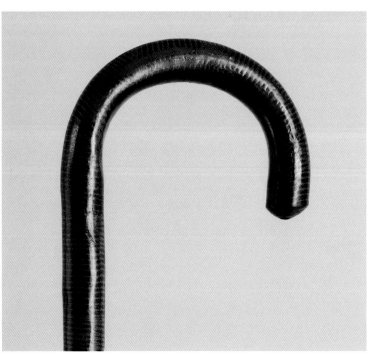

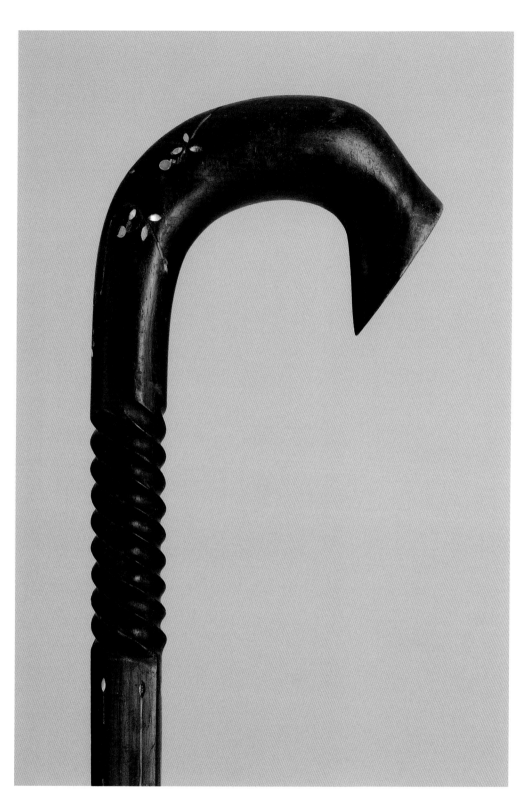

CA074

嵌螺鈿拐杖

木　長88公分、杖柄長12公分　20世紀

Mother-of-pearl-inlaid cane

Wood;　length 88 cm, length of handle 12 cm;　20th century

CA118

銀帽直身杖

銀、木　長88公分　20世紀

杖首包覆銀頭，刻「吉祥壽考」字樣，並刻有孝親圖。

Cane with silver cap handle

Silver, wood; length 88 cm; 20th century

The silver cap handle is inscribed with "Ji xiang shou kao" ("wishing one a long life") with images of filial piety.

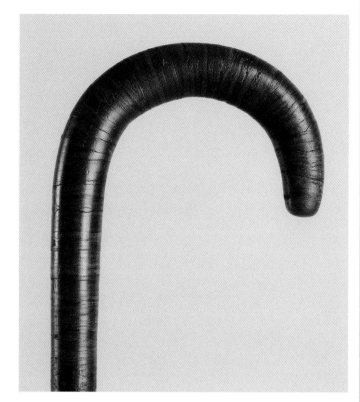

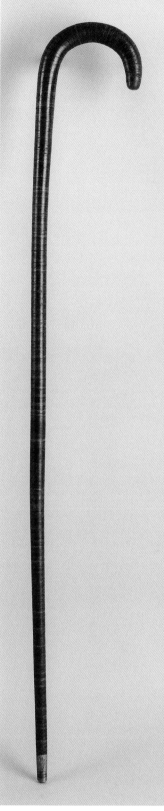

CA068

包藤皮手杖

藤、包藤皮　長88.5公分、杖柄長13公分　20世紀

Rattan cane wrapped in rattan skin

Rattan;　length 88.5 cm, length of handle 13 cm;　20th century

CA069

包竹皮手杖

竹皮漆胎、木　長87公分、杖柄長14公分　20世紀

Bamboo cane weaved with bamboo strips

Bamboo, wood;　length 87 cm, length of handle 14 cm;　20th century

CA066

癭瘤木杖

樹根　長115.5公分　20世紀

自然成形，佈滿樹瘤，有些癭瘤部分有加工雕刻。

Rattan cane with abnormal growths

Rattan; length 115.5 cm; 20th century

The cane utilizes the tree's natural shape and its abnormal growths.

CA067

鳥喙首木杖

木　長89.5公分　20世紀

未加雕刻，天然成形。

Cane with bird head-shaped handle

Wood; length 89.5 cm; 20th century

The cane utilizes the natural shape of the wood to create the bird head-shaped handle.

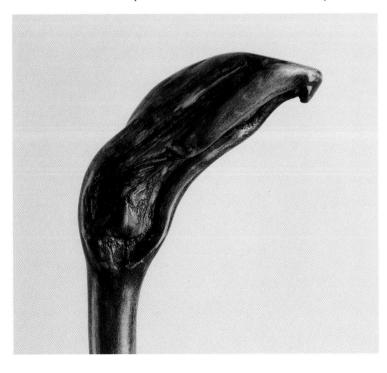

CA065

藤杖

藤　長90公分　20世紀

杖身爲整塊藤，未加雕飾。

Rattan cane

Rattan; length 90 cm; 20th century

The shaft is an entire piece of rattan, and it does not have any carvings.

CA064

藤杖

藤　長110公分、杖柄長16公分　20世紀

未加雕飾、杖身塗漆。

Rattan cane

Rattan; length 110 cm, length of handle 16 cm; 20th century

The cane does not have any carvings, and it is painted with lacquer.

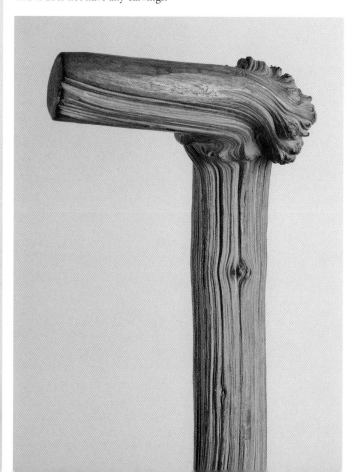

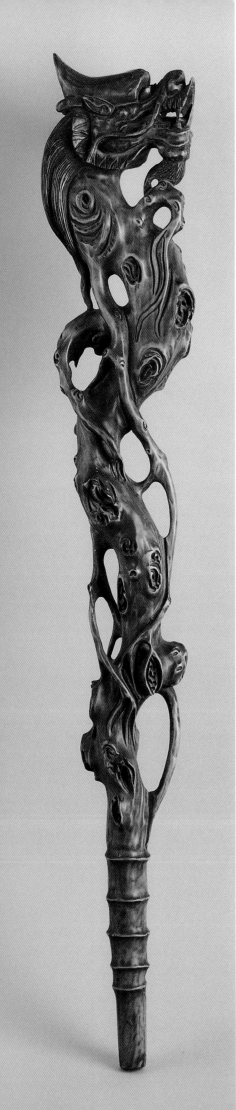

CA123

雕龍木杖

黃楊木　長90公分、杖柄長14公分　20世紀

Boxwood cane in the shape of a dragon

Boxwood; length 90 cm, length of handle 14 cm; 20th century

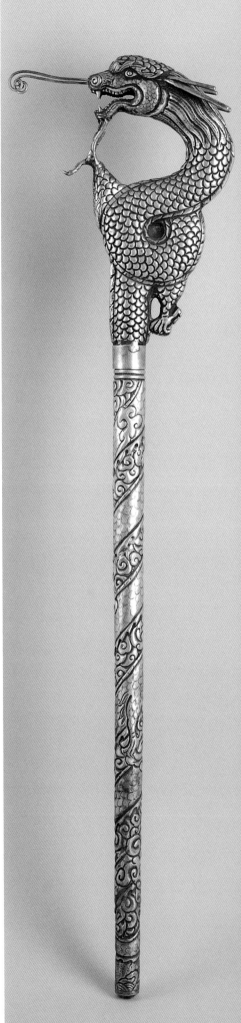

CA091

銀龍手杖

銀　長83公分　20世紀

Silver dragon cane

Silver; length 83 cm; 20th century

CA051

龍首木杖

木　長93公分、杖柄長16.5公分　20世紀

Dragon cane

Wood;　length 93 cm, length of handle 16.5 cm;　20th century

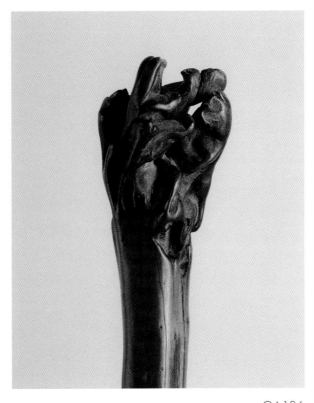

CA106
草桿杖
長90公分　20世紀
原產美國，百年生成之質地。

Grass cane
Length 90 cm; 20th century

CA061
竹節杖
竹、附牛角材質之鼻煙壺　長90公分　19世紀
杖身刻有「乃木□得同下一遺訓　萬山不重君思重
一髮不輕臣命輕　□山老人作」之字樣。

Bamboo cane with gourd
Bamboo; length 90 cm; 19th century

The shaft in inscribed with words.

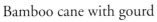

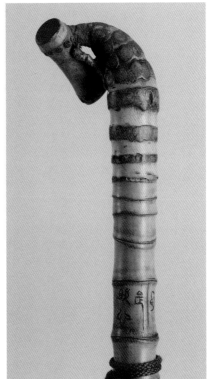

不只是杖具—杖具的特殊類型

杖具的實用性功能，是載負使用者重量，並且助其行走。然而從杖具工藝演變及文化意義來看，杖具，不只是杖具。許多杖具尚有不同功能，可說是一杖兩用或一杖多用。例如日本有所謂的「機關杖」，在杖內藏有各種物件，「手杖刀劍」則將刀劍置於杖身內，佩帶手杖刀劍甚至形成18世紀的一種歐洲流行風尚。

The cane's purpose is to support the user's weight and to help the user walk. However, through the evolution of cane-making and its cultural significance, the cane is not just a cane. The cane has many different functions; it can be dual-purposed or multi-purposed. For example, Japan has the so-called "gadget walking sticks" that has hidden gadgets inside the cane. Furthermore, the sword cane, which contains a sword in its shaft, was a popular accessory in eighteenth century Europe.

Sword Canes

手杖刀劍

手杖刀劍是介於兵器與暗器間的兵器。杖身中空，內藏窄身刀劍一把。杖柄即為刀柄，為便於抽刀刺敵之用，手杖刀劍的杖柄多為筆直的形狀，不似普通半彎形的杖柄。特別是18世紀後流行於歐洲的手杖刀劍，以各種形式呈現。

在中國古代，自皇帝到文人皆喜愛佩劍以顯示身份。在歐洲，劍被用於冊封爵士與騎士的象徵儀式上。然而劍在19世紀初已盡失優勢，被輕便的手槍替代，劍退出時尚的行列後，手杖代替了劍的位置，並且出現在手杖中隱藏的刀劍的設計，風行的程度如法國武術（La Canne）就是將藏有刀劍的手杖作為武器。

The sword cane is a type of weapon. The cane's shaft is hollow, where a narrow sword can be hidden. Meanwhile, the cane's handle converts into the hilt of the sword, allowing easy access when drawing the sword to kill an enemy due to the sword cane's straight handle, which is a contrast to the typical curved handles in ordinary canes. Particularly after the eighteenth century, the variety of sword canes increased with their rising popularity in Europe.

In Ancient China, from the emperor to scholars, everyone liked the saber because it represented status, while in Europe, the sword was used when bestowing a knight his rank and title. However, by the nineteenth century, the sword lost its superiority and was usurped by the simplistic gun. After the sword went out of fashion, the cane replaced the sword, and sword canes began emerging. Eventually, the sword cane even became a French martial arts weapon called La canne.

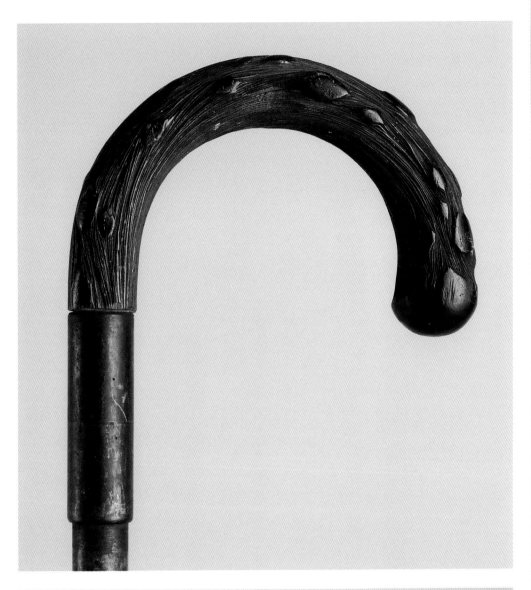

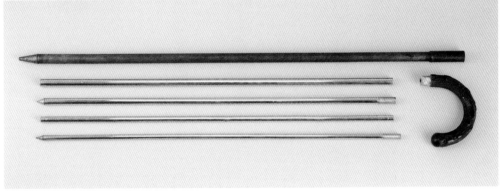

CA092

木柄金屬手杖

木、金屬　長89公分、杖柄長13公分、短125公分　20世紀

金屬杖身，木頭杖柄，內藏四支不鏽鋼短棍，兩兩可相拼接成一端為平口，另一端則帶有尖端可刺擊，類似「殳」形狀的兵器。

Cane with wooden handle

Wood (handle), metal (shaft); length 89 cm, length of handle 13 cm, length of spear 125 cm; 20th century

The shaft contains a hidden weapon, which is four pieces that can be assembled into two spears with pointed ends.

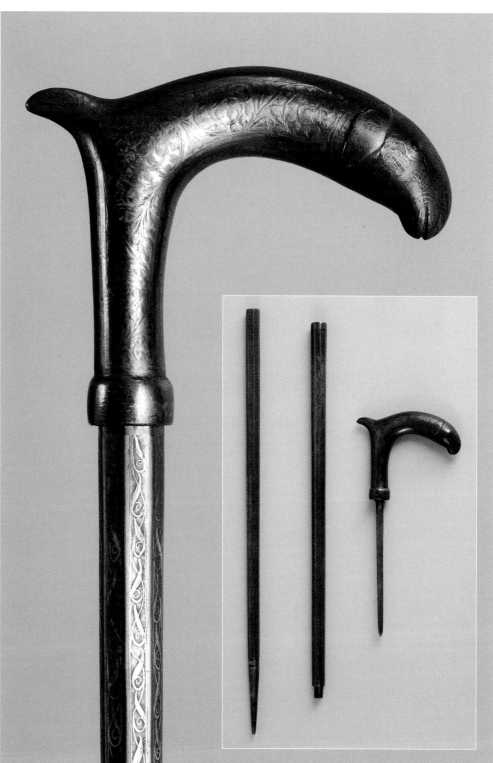

CA006

獸首柄手杖

銀、混合金屬　長90公分、杖柄長9公分　20世紀

杖具由三部份組合而成。整件裝飾花草紋，杖身內藏有短劍。

Silver cane with beast-shaped handle

Silver alloy; length 90 cm, length of handle 9 cm; 20th century

Cane consists of three parts. The entire cane is engraved with a floral pattern, and the shaft contains a hidden dagger.

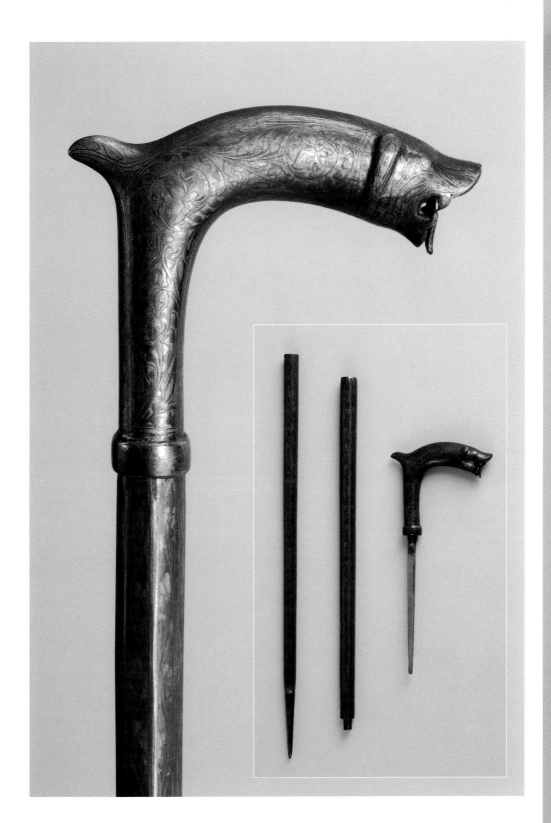

CA007

獸首柄手杖

銀、混合金屬　長92公分、杖柄長14公分　20世紀

杖具由三部份組合而成。整件裝飾有花草紋，杖柄頂端雕爲獸口，杖柄內藏有短劍。

Silver cane with beast-shaped handle

Silver alloy; length 92 cm, length of handle 14 cm; 20th century

Cane consists of three parts. The entire cane is engraved with a floral pattern, and the handle is carved in the shape of a beast's mouth. The shaft contains a hidden dagger.

CA008

獸頭銀手杖

銀、混合金屬　長95公分、杖柄長10公分　20世紀

杖具由三部份組合而成。整件裝飾有花草紋，杖柄頂端雕為獸口，杖柄內藏有短劍。

Silver cane with beast-shaped handle

Silver alloy;　length 95 cm, length of handle 10 cm;　20th century

Cane consists of three parts. The entire cane is engraved with a floral pattern, and the handle is carved in the shape of a beast's mouth.　The shaft contains a hidden dagger.

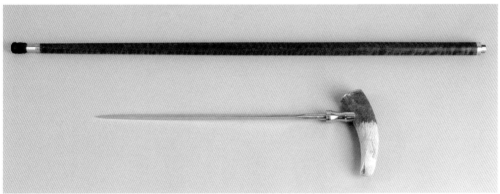

CA013

鷹首獸角柄木杖

獸角、金屬身、木紋貼皮　長90公分、杖柄長16公分、刃長40公分　20世紀

杖首依獸角形狀刻出老鷹，杖身內藏有短劍。

Cane with eagle head-shaped handle

Beast horn (handle), metal (shaft); length 90 cm, length of handle 16, length of blade 40 cm; 20th century

Handle is carved from a beast's horn in the shape of an eagle, and the shaft contains a hidden dagger.

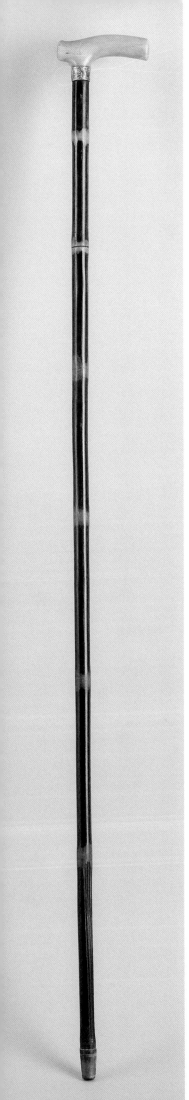

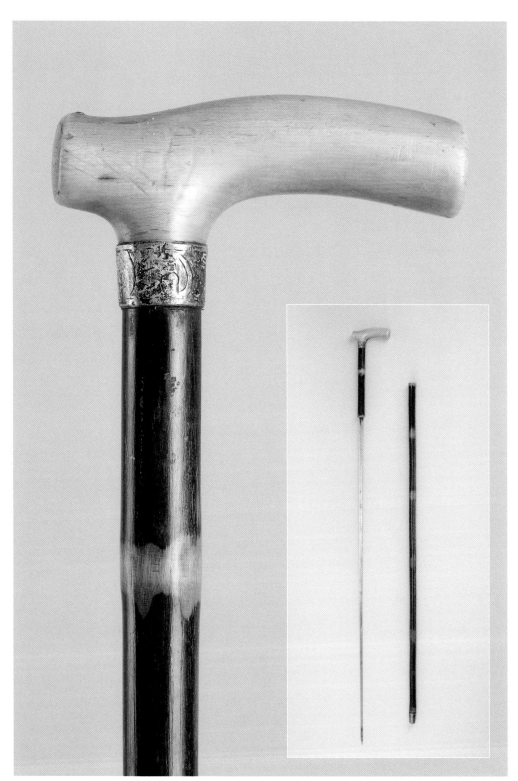

CA022

象牙柄竹杖

象牙、竹　長85公分、杖柄長7公分　20世紀

本件杖身內藏長劍。

Cane with ivory handle

Ivory (handle), bamboo (shaft); length 85 cm, length of handle 7 cm; 20th century

The shaft contains a sword.

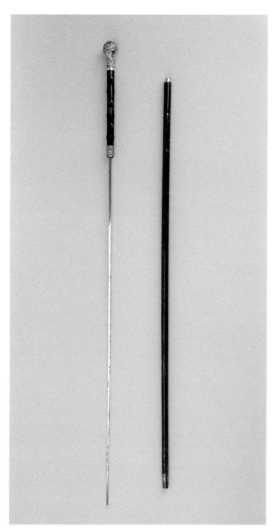

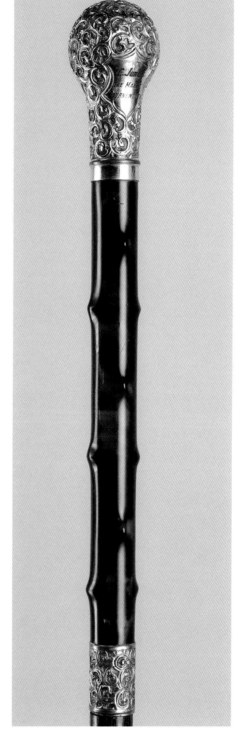

CA088

圓球首玳瑁柄手杖

金屬、玳瑁、木　長91公分，刃長62公分　20世紀

杖身內藏西洋劍。

Tortoise shell and wood cane with gold handle

Gold (handle), tortoise shell/wood (shaft); length 91 cm, length of blade 62 cm; 20th century

The shaft contains a rapier. E. Jones, The Manse Bournemouth.

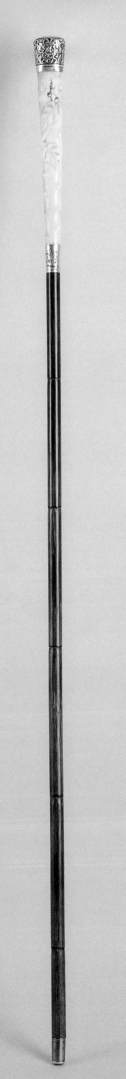

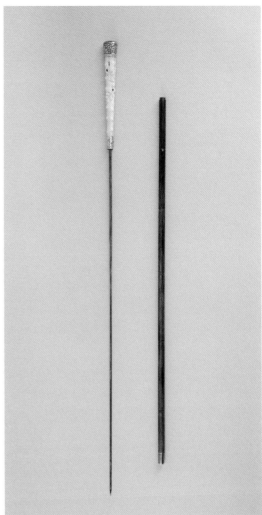

CA087

花卉紋飾象牙柄手杖

銀、象牙、木　長94.5公分，刃長70.5公分　20世紀

杖身爲木頭，仿竹節的形式，而杖身內藏西洋劍。杖首頂端刻有「P」與「L」組合之西洋花案字。

Cane carved with flower designs

Silver/ivory (handle), wood (shaft); length 94.5 cm, length of blade 70.5 cm; 20th century

The shaft is made from wood but it has the appearance of bamboo, and the shaft contains a rapier. The initials "P" and "L" are intertwined on the top of the handle.

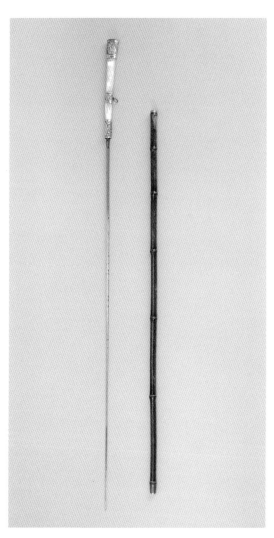

CA089

嵌金珍珠貝手杖

金屬、珍珠貝、竹　長90公分、刃長76公分　20世紀

杖身內藏西洋劍，杖首頂端刻「E、G　15□G.P.」之字樣。

Gold and mother-of-pearl cane

Gold, mother-of-pearl, bamboo; length 90 cm, length of blade 76 cm; 20th century

The shaft contains a rapier, and the top of the handle is inscribed with "E", "G", "15__G.P."

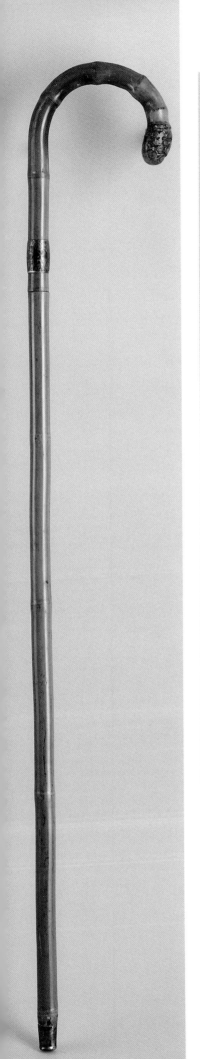

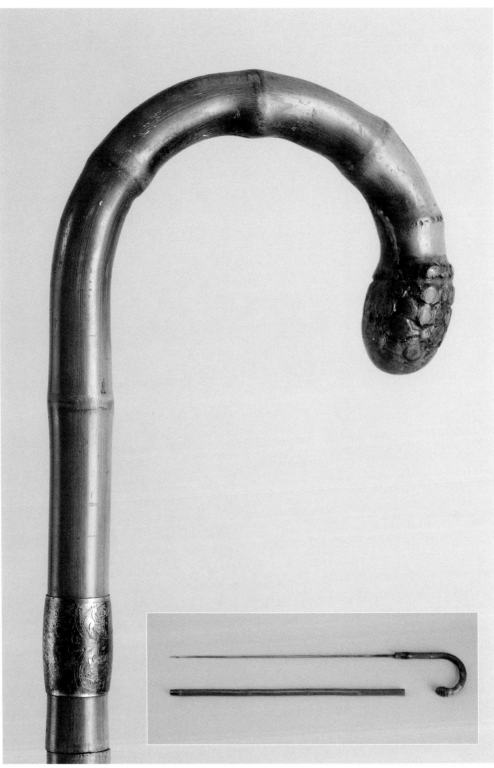

CA097

竹節手杖

銀環、竹　長94.5公分、杖柄長12公分、刃長70公分　20世紀

Bamboo cane

Bamboo; length 81 cm, length of handle 12 cm, length of blade 70 cm; 20th century

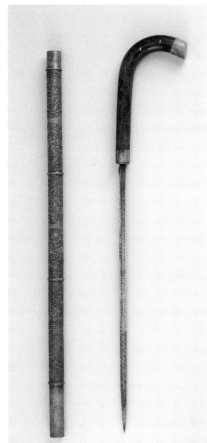

CA057

手杖刀

木、金屬　長90公分、杖柄長13公分、刃長50公分　20世紀

杖身內藏有短劍，柄刻有「伴我旅行良友　宣統元年作」字樣。

Cane with carvings and wooden handle

Wood (handle), metal (shaft); length 90 cm, length of handle 13 cm, length of blade 50 cm; 20th century

The metal cane's shaft contains a hidden dagger.

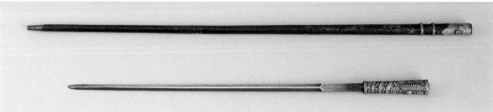

CA081

嵌珊瑚龍首杖

珊瑚、金屬　長90公分、刃長60公分　20世紀

Cane carved with dragon and inlaid with coral

Coral, metal;　length 90 cm, length of blade 60 cm;　20th century

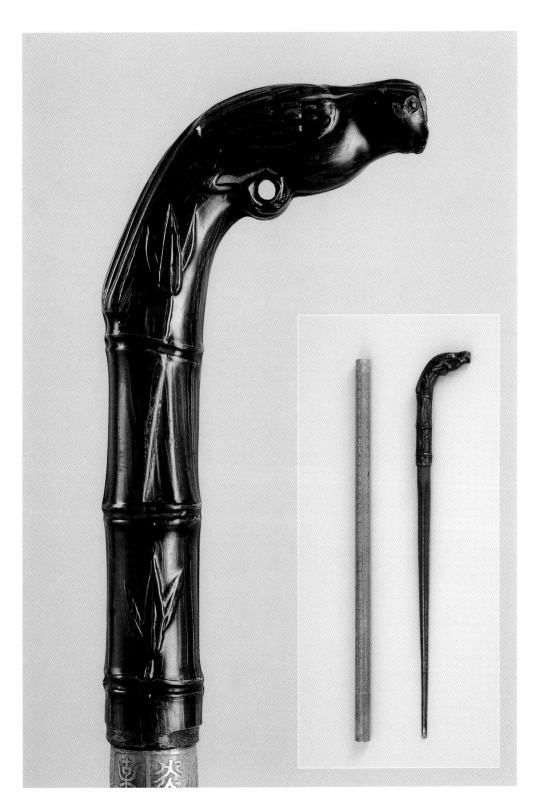

CA083

麻雀首柄手杖

木、金屬　長48公分、刃長31公分　20世紀

杖首刻為麻雀，麻雀喜歡親近人類，故常應用在中國各類藝術品中，本杖杖身內藏短劍，杖身刻滿福祿富貴等吉祥紋，可能為小王子或貴族使用。

Cane with wood sparrow-shaped handle

Wood (handle), metal (shaft); length 48 cm, length of blade 31 cm; 20th century

The handle is carved in the shape of a sparrow. Sparrows are friendly to human; thus, the image of sparrow is a popular one in Chinese art. The shaft contains a hidden dagger.

CA086

龍紋首金屬杖

金屬　長83公分 刃長34.5公分　20世紀

Metal dragon head-shaped handle cane

Metal; length 83 cm, length of blade 34.5 cm; 20th century

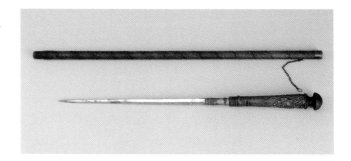

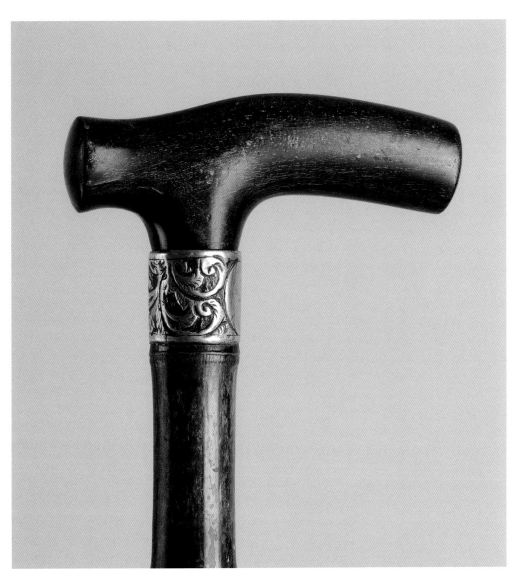

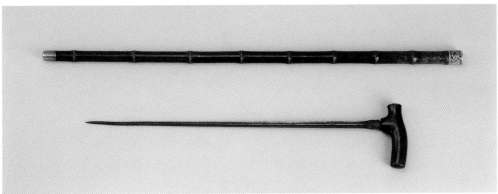

CA112
牛角柄竹節手杖
牛角、竹　長80公分、杖柄長11.5公分、刃長52公分　20世紀

Bamboo cane with cattle-horn handle
Cattle-horn (handle), bamboo (shaft); length 80 cm, length of handle 11.5 cm, length of blade 52 cm; 20th century

Gadget Canes

附件杖

除了倚靠支稱身體重量行走之外，添附了各種實用性功能，例如杖身內設置羅盤、望遠鏡、武器、煙盒、雨傘等具有一杖多用的特點。日本有所謂的「機關杖」（仕込み杖，Shikomizue），泛指內藏有其他物件的杖具，從機關杖外是無法看出有內藏物，亦有人藏過扇子、煙管等物件。在1876年日本明治時期，曾針對隨身攜帶的刀劍下過禁令，然而一般為了防身之用，機關杖內開始藏設刀劍，此類刀劍通常尺寸短小、形製單純，或是尖銳的針狀物。

Another type of cane is the "Gadget Canes" because in addition to supporting the user's body weight and helping the user walk, it also has several other functions. For instance, the shaft of the cane can contain: a compass, telescope, weapon, cigarette case, umbrella, etc, which provide the cane with a multi-purpose function. Japan has the so-called "gadget walking sticks" (仕込み杖, Shikomizue), and as a result, the name "gadget walking stick" has become the standard nomenclature. From the outside, the cane does not appear to possess any concealed objects, but people have hidden fans, smoking pipes, etc. In 1876, the Japanese Meiji government banned the carrying of swords by civilians; yet, to maintain self-defense, the Japanese people began concealing swords inside canes. Typically, swords that were hidden inside canes were short in length, simple in construction, or slender and sharply-pointed in shape.

CA103

煙嘴竹杖

竹、金屬配飾　長91公分、杖柄長14.5公分　20世紀

杖柄內部藏有煙管，便於攜帶，一杖兩用。

Cane with tobacco pipe

Bamboo;　length 91 cm, length of handle 14.5 cm;　20th century

The handle contains a tobacco pipe for convenience.

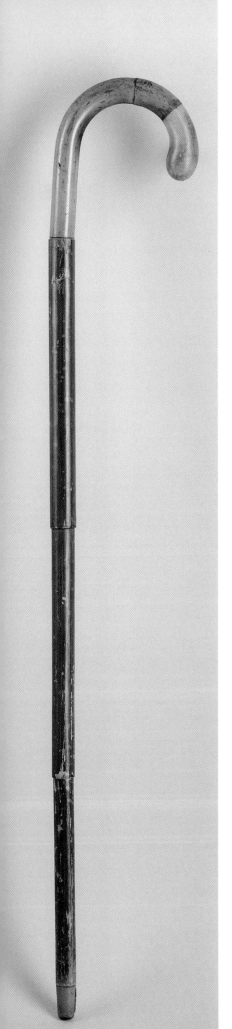

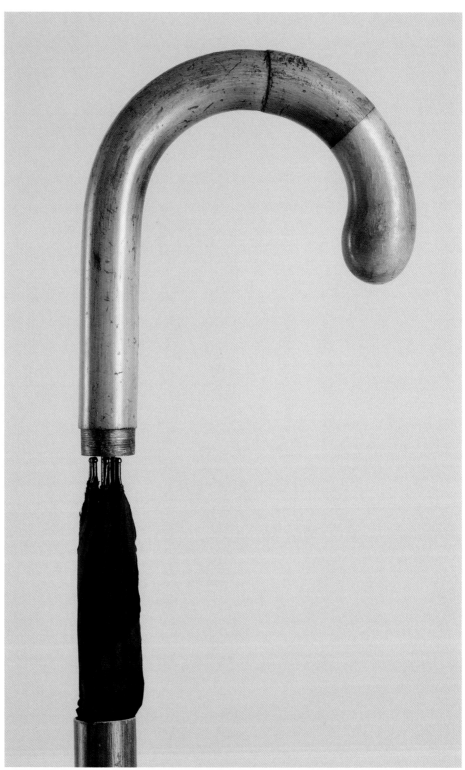

CA082

獸角柄帶傘手杖

獸角、竹、傘布傘骨　長89公分、杖柄長15公分　20世紀

杖身內藏雨傘，杖身由中空之竹子拼接而成。

Cane with beast horn handle and hidden umbrella

Beast horn (handle), bamboo (shaft); length 89 cm, length of handle 15 cm; 20th century

The shaft contains an umbrella, and the shaft is assembled from several bamboo pieces.

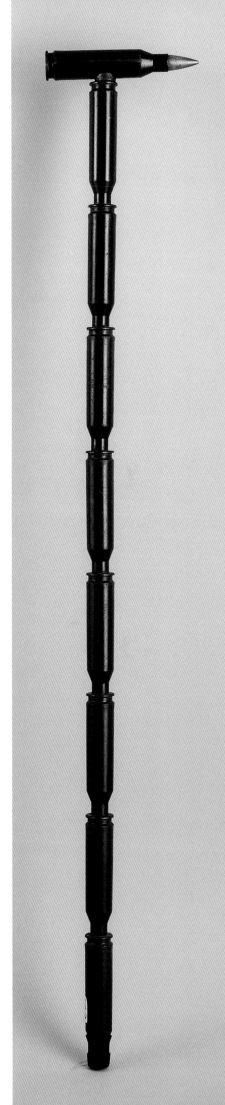

CA084

彈殼手杖

金屬　長90公分、杖柄長14公分　20世紀

全杖為彈殼拼接而成。

Bullet shells-shaped cane

Metal; length 90 cm, length of handle 14 cm; 20th century

The cane is assembled from metal bullet-shaped pieces.

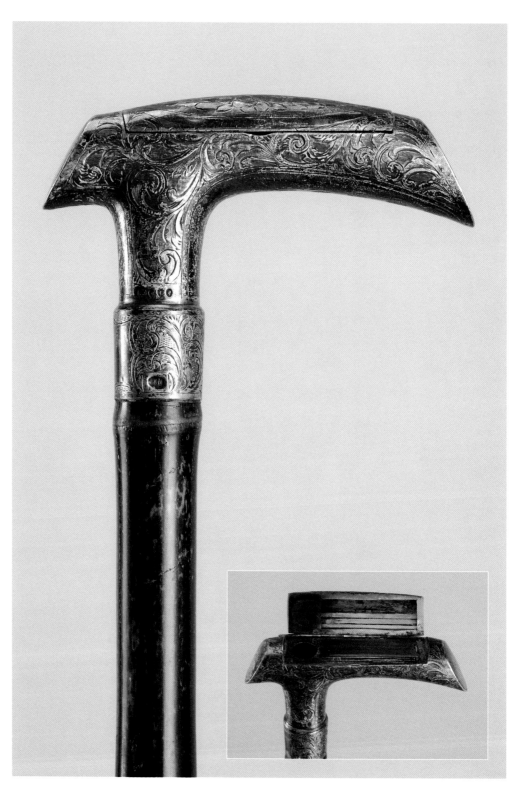

CA085

銀柄手杖

金屬、竹　長90公分　20世紀

杖頭內藏有火柴盒、雪茄收納盒。

Cane with silver handle and hidden cigarettes/matches compartment

Metal (handle), bamboo (shaft); length 90 cm; 20th century

The handle contains a hidden compartment for cigarettes and matches.

112

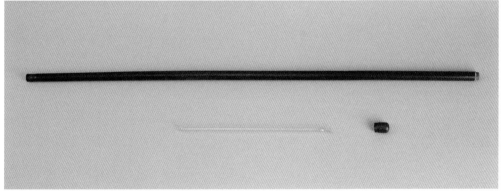

CA098

直身木杖

木 長90公分、玻璃管長29公分，寬1.2公分 20世紀

杖身內有透明玻璃管，可作爲藏酒處，便於隨身攜帶。

Wooden cane with hidden glass tubes

Wood; length 90 cm, length of glass tube 29 cm, width 1.2 cm; 20th century

The shaft contains hidden glass tubes that were probably used to hold alcohol.

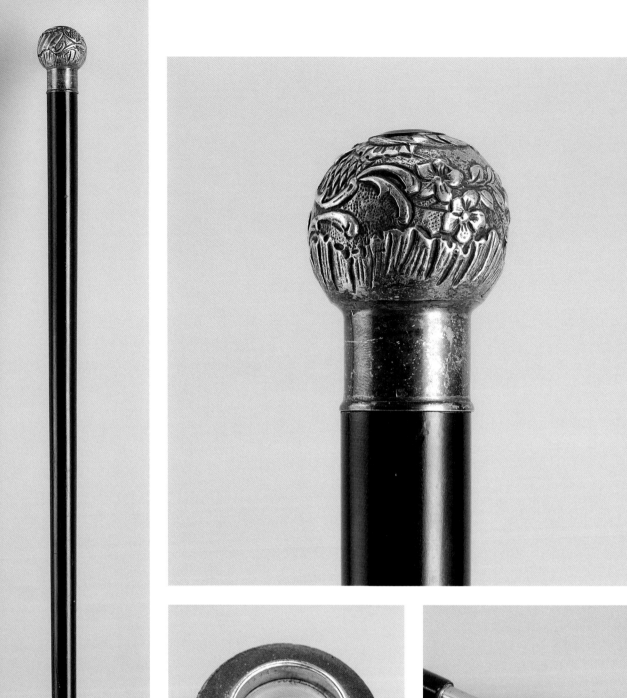

CA105

指南針與望遠鏡手杖

銀、木　長93公分　20世紀

Cane with hidden telescope and compass

Silver, wood;　length 93 cm;　20th century

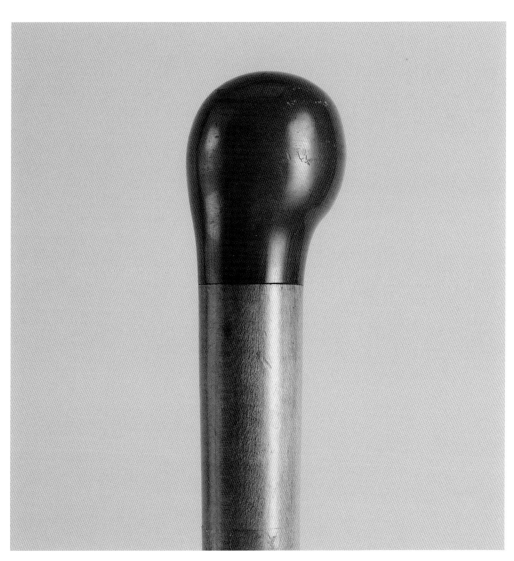

CA104

古董手電筒手杖

木　長94公分　20世紀

杖首內藏有古董小燈泡，轉動金屬環為開關，則有手電筒的功能。

Cane with antique flashlight

Wood; length 94 cm; 20th century

The handle contains an antique flashlight. Turn the cane's collar to turn on the flashlight.

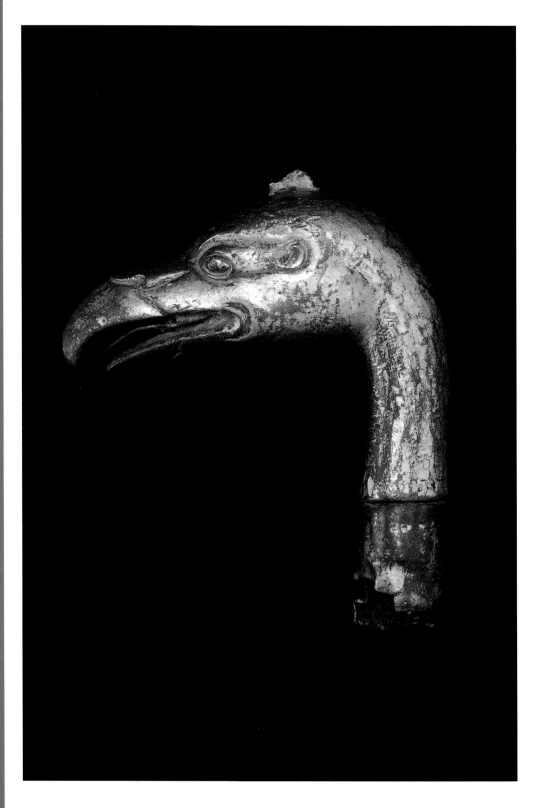

CA130

鐵鋈金鷹首柄

鐵、鋈金　10×8.5公分　約16世紀

Iron handle with gold-leafing

Iron, gold leaf;　10×8.5 cm;　c. 16th century

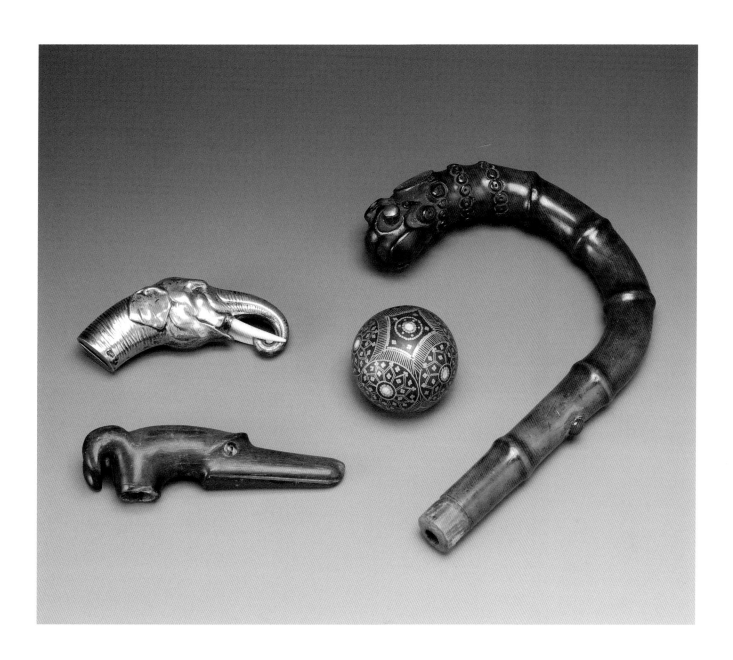

CA128

各式杖柄

（右一）竹根杖柄15.5×13公分　　（右二）木嵌銀絲杖柄 4×4.4公分
（左上）銀鑲嵌象牙杖柄7×6公分　　（左下）木雕犬首杖柄2.8×10.3公分

Handles

From right to left: Bamboo root handle- 15.5x13 cm; Wood handle inlaid with silver thread- 4x4.4 cm; Silver handle inlaid with ivory- 7x6 cm; Handle with dog head carving- 2.8x10.3 cm

CA125

象牙杖柄

（右一）6.2×2.8公分　　（右二）7.6×3.1公分　　（右三）8.2×3.5公分
（右四）11.8×4.9公分　　（右五）6×5公分　　（右六）3.8×3.8公分

Ivory handles

From right to left (6.2×2.8 cm, 7.6×3.1 cm, 8.2×3.5 cm, 11.8×4.9 cm, 6×5 cm, 3.8×3.8 cm)

CA126

玉巧雕杖柄

（右一）4.5×4.5公分　（右二）4.6×6.4公分　（右三）5×5公分
（右四）7.3×4公分　（右五）5×4.5公分

Jade handles

From right to left (4.5×4.5 cm, 4.6×6.4 cm, 5×5 cm, 7.3×4 cm, 5×4.5 cm)

CA127

玉巧雕杖柄

（右一）8.5×1.8公分　　（右二）10.3×6公分
（右三）12.6×4.4公分　　（右四）8.2×2.7公分

Jade handles

From right to left (8.5×1.8 cm, 10.3×6 cm, 12.6×4.4 cm, 8.2×2.7 cm)

CA129

玉杖柄

後：（右一）4.8×3.2公分　　（右二）7.8×2.5公分　　（右三）10×2.7公分
　　（右四）10.3×2.5公分　（右五）6.6×3.3公分　（右六）5.1×2.5公分

前：（右一）3.6×2.5公分　　（右二）4×3.7公分　　（右三）5.1×3.1公分
　　（右四）2.8×3.6公分　　（右五）3.6×2.5公分

Jade handles

Back- from right to left (4.8×3.2 cm, 7.8×2.5 cm, 10×2.7 cm, 10.3×2.5 cm, 6.6×3.3 cm, 5.1×2.5 cm)

Front- from right to left (3.6×2.5 cm, 4×3.7 cm, 5.1×3.1 cm, 2.8×3.6 cm, 3.6×2.5 cm)

作品索引
List of Plates

CA001 P.44
人面銀首竹杖
銀首、竹身 長90公分
20世紀
Cane with silver human face-shaped handle
Silver (handle), wood (shaft); length 90 cm; 20th century

CA002 P.46
鴨首木杖
木首、金屬環 長94公分、杖柄長13公分 20世紀
Cane with duck head-shaped handle
Wood; length 94 cm, length of handle 13 cm; 20th century

CA003 P.46
鳥首杖
木 長94公分 20世紀
Cane with bird-shaped handle
Wood; length 94 cm; 20th century

CA004 P.47
龍首杖
木 長102公分 20世紀
Cane with dragon-shaped handle
Wood; length 102 cm; 20th century

CA005 P.47
鳳首杖
木 長84.5公分、杖柄長13公分 20世紀
Cane with phoenix-shaped handle
Wood; length 84.5 cm, length of handle 13 cm; 20th century

CA006 P.94
獸首柄手杖
銀、混合金屬 長90公分、杖柄長9公分 20世紀
Silver cane with beast-shaped handle
Silver alloy; length 90 cm, length of handle 9 cm; 20th century

CA007 P.95
獸首柄手杖
銀、混合金屬 長92公分、杖柄長14公分 20世紀
Silver cane with beast-shaped handle
Silver alloy; length 92 cm, length of handle 14 cm; 20th century

CA008 P.96
獸頭銀首手杖
銀、混合金屬 長95公分、杖柄長10公分 20世紀
Silver cane with beast-shaped handle
Silver alloy; length 95 cm, length of handle 10 cm; 20th century

CA009 P.48
獅首杖
木、金屬環 長87公分、杖柄長12公分 20世紀
Cane with lion-shaped handle
Wood; length 87 cm, length of handle 12 cm; 20th century

CA010 P.45
犬首杖
銀首、竹身 長85公分、杖柄長10公分 20世紀
Cane with silver dog head-shaped handle
Silver (handle), bamboo (shaft); length 85 cm, length of handle 10 cm; 20th century

CA011 P.48
鷹首牛角柄木杖
牛角柄、金屬環、木身 長80公分 20世紀
Cane with eagle-shaped handle
Cattle horn (handle), wood (shaft); length 80 cm; 20th century

CA012 P.36
犬首鹿角柄木杖
鹿角柄、金屬環、木身 長90公分 1870年
Cane with dog head-shaped handle
Stag antler (handle), ebony (shaft); length 90 cm; 1870

CA013 P.97
鷹首獸角柄木杖
獸角、金屬環、木紋貼皮 長90公分 20世紀
Cane with eagle head-shaped handle
Beast horn (handle), metal (shaft); length 90 cm; 20th century

CA014 P.50
犬首斑竹手杖
象牙、銀環、斑竹身 長77公分 20世紀
Cane with dog head-shaped handle
Ivory (handle), bamboo (shaft); length 77 cm; 20th century

CA015 P.50
麒麟柄牙竹杖
象牙、銀、竹身 長88公分 19世紀
Cane with Kilin-shaped handle
Ivory (handle), bamboo (shaft); length 88 cm; 19th century

CA016 P.32
犬首象牙杖
象牙、金屬環 長88.5公分、刃長46公分 20世紀
Cane with dog head-shaped handle
Ivory; length 88.5 cm, length of sword 46 cm; 20th century

CA017 P.33
圓球首龍紋象牙杖
象牙 長94.5公分、杖柄寬度5公分 19世紀
Cane with dragon designs and round handle
Ivory; length 94.5 cm, width of handle 5 cm; 19th century

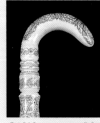

CA018 P.34
象牙手杖
象牙 長94公分、杖柄長11.5公分 20世紀
Cane with Indian pattern designs
Ivory; length 94 cm, length of handle 11.5 cm; 20th century

CA019 P.23
羚羊角串果實木杖
羚羊角、非洲果實 長87公分 20世紀
Antelope horn and African fruit cane
Antelope horn, African fruit; length 87 cm; 20th century

CA020 P.38
羚羊角柄木杖
羚羊角、羊蹄、木 長84.5公分 20世紀
Cane with antelope horn handle
Antelope horn (handle), antelope hoof (collar), wood (shaft); length 84.5 cm; 20th century

CA021 P.37
獸牙柄木杖
野豬牙、木 長89公分、杖柄長11.5公分 20世紀
Cane with boar tusk handle
Boar tusk (handle), wood (shaft); length 89 cm, length of handle 11.5 cm; 20th century

CA022 P.98
象牙柄竹杖
象牙、竹 長85公分、杖柄長7公分 20世紀
Cane with ivory handle
Ivory (handle), bamboo (shaft); length 85 cm, length of handle 7 cm; 20th century

CA023 P.37
象牙柄木杖
象牙、木 長87公分、杖柄長12公分 20世紀
Cane with ivory handle
Ivory (handle), wood (shaft); length 87 cm, length of handle 12 cm; 20th century

CA024 P.55

包金柄竹杖

金、竹 長84公分 20世紀

Cane with gold handle

Gold (handle), bamboo (shaft); length 84 cm; 20th century

CA025 P.49

銀柄西洋杖

銀、木 長88公分、杖柄長12公分 約1890年

Cane with silver handle

Silver (handle), wood (shaft); length 88 cm, length of handle 12 cm; c. 1890

CA026 P.53

銅杖

銅 長88公分、杖柄長12公分 20世紀

Bronze cane

Bronze; length 88 cm, length of handle 12 cm; 20th century

CA027 P.53

銀包柄竹節杖

竹、銀 長89公分、杖柄長14公分 1909年

Cane with silver handle

Silver (handle), bamboo (shaft); length 89 cm, length of handle 14 cm; 1909

CA028 P.43

琺瑯柄西洋手杖

金屬、木 長92公分、杖柄長14公分 20世紀

Cane with enamel handle

Enamel (handle), wood (shaft); length 92 cm, length of handle 14 cm; 20th century

CA030 P.54

包金首玳瑁杖

金、玳瑁 長90公分 20世紀

Tortoise shell cane with gold handle

Gold (handle), tortoise shell (shaft); length 90 cm; 20th century

CA031 P.24

日本銀箍首木杖

銀、木 長88公分 19世紀

Cane with Japanese Metal handle

Silver (handle), wood (shaft); length 88 cm; Late 19th century

CA032 P.56

扁銅球首直身杖

銅首、木身 長109.5公分、杖柄長5公分 20世紀

Cane with flat, round handle

Bronze (handle), wood (shaft); length 109.5 cm, length of handle 5 cm; 20th century

CA033 P.18

西班牙家徽紋藤杖

金屬鑲嵌、鐵、藤 長86公分 約1870年

Spanish Malika rattan cane

Metal, iron, rattan; length 86 cm; c. 1870

CA034 P.56

包銀首直身木杖

象牙、銀、木 長95公分 20世紀

Cane with silver handle

Silver (handle), ivory/wood (shaft); length 95 cm; 20th century

CA035 P.57

象牙首木質手杖

象牙、銀、木 長86公分、杖柄長4公分 20世紀

Cane with ivory handle

Ivory (handle), wood (shaft); length 86 cm, length of handle 4 cm; 20th century

CA036 P.57

象牙球首木杖

象牙、琥珀、木 長102公分 20世紀

Tortoise shell cane with ivory, round handle

Ivory (handle), tortoise shell/ rattan (shaft); length 102 cm; 20th century

CA037 P.16

俄羅斯手杖

金屬、木 長88公分 約1880年

Russian cane with silver and niello handle

Silver and niello (handle), ebony (shaft); length 88 cm; c. 1880

CA038 P.20

包編織幾何紋手杖

編織表面 長88公分 1888年

Woven-covered cane

Woven-covered; length 88 cm; 1888

CA039 P.21

幾何紋竹杖

竹 長103公分 20世紀

Cane with carved patterns

Bamboo; length 103 cm; 20th century

CA040 P.22

夫妻杖

木 長84.5公分、杖柄長13公分 20世紀

Man and woman cane

Wood; length 84.5 cm, length of handle 13 cm; 20th century

CA041 P.54

嵌銀幾何紋直身杖

木、銀絲 長89公分 20世紀

Silver-inlaid cane

Wood, silver thread; length 89 cm; 20th century

CA042 P.62

鳥形柄蛇身手杖

木 長92公分、杖柄長20公分 20世紀

Cane carved with bird, humans, and snake

Wood; length 92 cm, length of handle 20 cm; 20th century

CA043 P.63

仙翁樹瘤杖

木 長90公分 19世紀

God of Longevity cane

Wood; length 90 cm; 19th century

CA044 P.64

翁首樹瘤杖

木、塗漆 長115公分 20世紀

God of Longevity cane

Red lacquer wood; length 115 cm; 20th century

CA045 P.65

翁首八仙杖

木、塗漆 長124公分 20世紀

The Eight Immortals cane

Lacquer wood; length 124 cm; 20th century

CA046 P.64

翁首詩文竹杖

竹 長96公分 20世紀

Cane with inscription and aged man-shaped handle

Bamboo; length 96 cm; 20th century

CA047 P.69

獸首人形木杖

木 長120公分 19世紀

Eight Trigrams cane

Wood; length 120 cm; 19th century

CA048 P.66

獅首杖

木 長98公分、杖柄長10公分 20世紀

Cane with lion-shaped handle

Wood; length 98 cm, length of handle 10 cm; 20th century

CA049　　　　P.67
松下封侯杖
黃楊木樹根　長122公分
20世紀

"Monkeys playing under
pine tree" cane
Wood; length 122 cm;
20th century

CA050　　　　P.66
猴首木杖
木　長119公分　20世紀

"Monkey drinking from
gourd" cane
Wood; length 119 cm;
20th century

CA051　　　　P.90
龍首木杖
木　長93公分、杖柄長
16.5公分　20世紀

Dragon cane
Wood; length 93 cm,
length of handle 16.5
cm; 20th century

CA052　　　　P.68
犬首木杖
木　長87公分、杖柄長18
公分　20世紀

Cane with dog head-
shaped handle
Wood; length 87 cm,
length of handle 18 cm;
20th century

CA053　　　　P.67
猴首蛇身杖
木　長100公分、杖柄長12
公分　20世紀

Monkey and snake
cane
Wood; length 100 cm,
length of handle 12 cm;
20th century

CA054　　　　P.80
木藤杖
木藤　長107公分、杖柄長
12公分　20世紀

Cane with inscriptions
and carvings
Wood; length 107 cm,
length of handle 12 cm;
20th century

CA055　　　　P.26
花鳥紋竹杖
竹　長88公分　20世紀

Cane carved with
flowers and birds
Bamboo; length 88 cm;
20th century

CA056　　　　P.26
花鳥紋竹杖
竹　長88.5公分　20世紀

Cane carved with pine
trees and cranes
Bamboo; length 88.5
cm; 20th century

CA057　　　　P.103
手杖刀
木、金屬　長90公分、刃
長50公分　20世紀

Cane with carvings and
wooden handle
Wood (handle), metal
(shaft); length 90 cm,
length of blade 50 cm;
20th century

CA058　　　　P.68
萬事如意杖
樹藤　長114公分　20世紀

"Wan shi ru yi" cane
Rattan; length 114 cm;
20th century

CA059　　　　P.73
嵌銀絲百壽杖
木、銀鑲嵌　長87公分、
杖柄長11公分　20世紀

Cane inlaid with one
hundred "shou"
Wood with silver inlay;
length 87 cm, length of
handle 11 cm; 20th
century

CA060　　　　P.70
竹節鳴蟬杖
黃楊木　長94公分、杖柄
長12公分　20世紀

Bamboo-shaped cane
with a carved cicada
Wood; length 94 cm,
length of handle 12 cm;
20th century

CA061　　　　P.91
竹節杖
竹、附牛角材質之鼻煙壺
長90公分　19世紀

Bamboo cane with
gourd
Bamboo; length 90 cm;
19th century

CA062　　　　P.72
竹節手杖
竹　長85.5公分、杖柄長
12公分　20世紀

Bamboo cane
Bamboo; length 85.5
cm, length of handle 12
cm; 20th century

CA063　　　　P.72
竹節手杖
竹　長86公分、杖柄長
14.5公分　20世紀

Bamboo cane
Bamboo; length 86 cm,
length of handle 14.5
cm; 20th century

CA064　　　　P.87
藤杖
藤　長110公分、杖柄長16
公分　20世紀

Rattan cane
Rattan; length 110 cm,
length of handle 16 cm;
20th century

CA065　　　　P.87
藤杖
藤　長90公分　20世紀

Rattan cane
Rattan; length 90 cm;
20th century

CA066　　　　P.86
瘤瘤木杖
樹根　長115.5公分　20世
紀

Rattan cane with
abnormal growths
Rattan; length 115.5
cm; 20th century

CA067　　　　P.86
鳥喙首木杖
木　長89.5公分　20世紀

Cane with bird head-
shaped handle
Wood; length 89.5 cm;
20th century

CA068　　　　P.85
包藤皮手杖
藤、包藤皮　長88.5公分、
杖柄長13公分　20世紀

Rattan cane wrapped in
rattan skin
Rattan; length 88.5 cm,
length of handle 13 cm;
20th century

CA069　　　　P.85
包竹皮手杖
竹皮漆胎、木　長87公
分、杖柄長14公分　20世
紀

Bamboo cane weaved
with bamboo strips
Bamboo, wood; length
87 cm, length of handle
14 cm; 20th century

CA070　　　　P.74
金首文人杖
金、木　長85公分　19世
紀

Cane with carvings and
gold handle
Gold (handle), wood
(shaft); length 85 cm;
19th century

CA071　　　　P.76
玉首蛇皮杖
蛇皮、竹　長62公分　約
1940年

Bamboo cane wrapped
in snake skin with jade
handle
Jade (handle), snake
skin/bamboo (shaft);
length 62 cm; Japanese
colonial period (1895-1945)

CA072　　　　P.75
玉龍首雲紋手杖
玉、紫檀木　長92公分、
杖柄長8公分　20世紀

Cane with jade dragon-
shaped handle
Jade (handle), wood
(shaft); length 92 cm,
length of handle 8 cm;
20th century

CA073 P.82
漆杖
漆身木胎 長92公分、杖
柄長6公分 20世紀
Cane with red lacquer handle
Wood; length 92 cm, length of handle 6 cm; 20th century

CA074 P.83
嵌螺鈿拐杖
木 長88公分、杖柄長12公分 20世紀
Mother-of-pearl-inlaid cane
Wood; length 88 cm, length of handle 12 cm; 20th century

CA075 P.78
獸足骨杖
獸足、木 長95公分 20世紀
Crane bone cane
Crane bone, wood; length 95 cm; 20th century

CA076 P.35
象牙杖
象牙 長87公分 20世紀
Ivory cane
Ivory; length 87 cm; 20th century

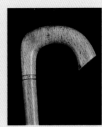

CA077 P.35
象牙手杖
象牙 長87公分、杖柄長12.5公分 20世紀
Ivory cane
Ivory; length 87 cm, length of handle 12.5 cm; 20th century

CA078 P.77
鹿角柄木杖
鹿角、金屬環、木 長88公分 20世紀
Cane with stag horn handle
Stag horn (handle), wood (shaft); length 88 cm; 20th century

CA079 P.77
鳥首文人杖
象牙、木 長83.5公分、杖柄長5公分 20世紀
Cane with bird head-shaped handle
Ivory (handle), wood (shaft); length 83.5 cm, length of handle 5 cm; 20th century

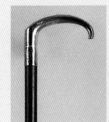

CA080 P.76
銀柄壽杖
金屬、紫檀木 長88公分、杖柄長9公分 20世紀
Cane with carvings and silver handle
Silver (handle), wood (shaft); length 88 cm, length of handle 9 cm; 20th century

CA081 P.104
嵌珊瑚龍首杖
珊瑚、金屬 長90公分、刃長60公分 20世紀
Cane carved with dragon and inlaid with coral
Coral, metal; length 90 cm, length of blade 60 cm; 20th century

CA082 P.110
獸角柄帶傘手杖
獸角、竹、傘布傘骨 長89公分 20世紀
Cane with beast horn handle and hidden umbrella
Beast horn (handle), bamboo (shaft); length 89 cm; 20th century

CA083 P.105
麻雀首柄手杖
木、金屬 長48公分、刃長31公分 20世紀
Cane with wood sparrow-shaped handle
Wood (handle), metal (shaft); length 48 cm, length of blade 31 cm; 20th century

CA084 P.111
彈殼手杖
金屬 長90公分、杖柄長14公分 20世紀
Bullet shells-shaped cane
Metal; length 90 cm, length of handle 14 cm; 20th century

CA085 P.112
銀柄手杖
金屬、竹 長90公分 20世紀
Cane with silver handle and hidden cigarettes/matches compartment
Metal (handle), bamboo (shaft); length 90 cm; 20th century

CA086 P.106
龍紋首金屬杖
金屬 長83公分 刃長34.5公分 20世紀
Metal dragon head-shaped handle cane
Metal; length 83 cm, length of blade 34.5 cm; 20th century

CA087 P.100
花卉紋飾象牙柄手杖
銀、象牙、木 長94.5公分、刃長70.5公分 20世紀
Cane carved with flower designs
Silver/ivory (handle), wood (shaft); length 94.5 cm, length of blade 70.5 cm; 20th century

CA088 P.99
圓球首玳瑁柄手杖
金屬、玳瑁、木 長91公分，刃長62公分 20世紀
Tortoise shell and wood cane with gold handle
Gold (handle), tortoise shell/wood (shaft); length 91 cm, length of blade 62 cm; 20th century

CA089 P.101
嵌金珍珠貝手杖
金屬、珍珠貝、竹 長90公分 20世紀
Gold and mother-of-pearl cane
Gold, mother-of-pearl, bamboo; length 90 cm; 20th century

CA090 P.17
銀柄扁球首手杖
銀、竹 長103公分、刃長75公分 1832年
Cane with silver, flat, round handle
Silver (handle), bamboo (shaft); length 103 cm, length of blade 75 cm; 1832

CA091 P.89
銀龍手杖
銀 長83公分 20世紀
Silver dragon cane
Silver; length 83 cm; 20th century

CA092 P.93
木柄金屬手杖
木、金屬 長89公分、杖柄長13公分、短125公分 20世紀
Cane with wooden handle
Wood (handle), metal (shaft); length 89 cm, length of handle 13 cm, length of spear 125 cm; 20th century

CA093 P.40
獅首獨角鯨牙權杖
金屬、獨角鯨牙 長149公分 20世紀
Narwhal tusk cane
Metal (handle), Narwhal tusk (shaft); length 149 cm; 20th century

CA094 P.55
花紋銀柄木杖
銀、木 長94.5公分、杖柄長12公分 20世紀
Cane with silver, floral designs handle
Silver (handle), wood (shaft); length 94.5 cm, length of handle 12 cm; 20th century

CA095 P.51
銅鴨首木杖
木、包金絲 長86公分、杖柄長8.5公分 20世紀
Gold-inlaid spiral cane with duck head-shaped handle
Bronze (handle), wood/gold (shaft); length 86 cm, length of handle 8.5 cm; 20th century

CA096 P.51
銅龍首木杖
木、包金絲 長86公分、杖柄長10.5公分 20世紀
Gold-inlaid spiral cane with dragon-shaped handle
Bronze (handle), wood/gold (shaft); length 86 cm, length of handle 10.5 cm; 20th century

CA097　　　　P.102
竹節手杖
銀環、竹　長94.5公分、杖
柄長12公分、刃長70公分
20世紀
Bamboo cane
Bamboo; length 81 cm,
length of handle 12 cm,
length of blade 70 cm;
20th century

CA098　　　　P.113
直身木杖
木　長90公分、玻璃管長
29公分　20世紀
**Wooden cane with
hidden glass tubes**
Wood; length 90 cm,
length of glass tube 29
cm; 20th century

CA099　　　　P.38
玳瑁首木杖
玳瑁、金屬環、木　長86.5
公分　1910年
**Cane with tortoise shell
handle**
Tortoise shell (handle),
wood (shaft); length
86.5 cm; 1910

CA100　　　　P.70
竹節鳴蟬杖
黃楊木　長80.5公分、杖柄
長11公分　20世紀
**Wood cane carved with
cicada**
Boxwood; length 80.5
cm, length of handle 11
cm; 20th century

CA101　　　　P.82
漆杖
黑漆木胎　長92公分、杖
柄長11.5公分　20世紀
**Red-on-black lacquer
cane**
Wood; length 92 cm,
length of handle 11.5
cm; 20th century

CA102　　　　P.27
竹杖
竹　長91公分、杖柄長
14.5公分　20世紀
Bamboo cane
Bamboo; length 91 cm,
length of handle 14.5
cm; 20th century

CA103　　　　P.109
煙嘴竹杖
竹、金屬配節　長91公
分、杖柄長14.5公分　20
世紀
Cane with tobacco pipe
Bamboo; length 91 cm,
length of handle 14.5
cm; 20th century

CA104　　　　P.115
古董手電筒手杖
木　長94公分　20世紀
**Cane with antique
flashlight**
Wood; length 94 cm;
20th century

CA105　　　　P.114
指南針與望遠鏡手杖
銀、木　長93公分　20世
紀
**Cane with hidden
telescope and compass**
Silver, wood; length 93
cm; 20th century

CA106　　　　P.91
草桿杖
長90公分　20世紀
Grass cane
Length 90 cm; 20th
century

CA107　　　　P.81
四方直身杖
象牙、黑漆木胎、獸角
長92公分　20世紀
**Cane with ivory,
squared handle**
Ivory (handle), ebony
(shaft), beast horn
(ferrule/tip); length 92
cm; 20th century

CA108　　　　P.42
羚羊角杖
羚羊角　長90公分、杖柄
長10公分　20世紀
**Cane with antelope
horn handle**
Antelope horn (handle),
wood (shaft); length 90
cm, length of handle 10
cm; 20th century

CA109　　　　P.39
羚羊角杖
羚羊角、藤　長86公分、
杖柄長11公分　20世紀
**Cane with antelope
horn handle**
Antelope horn (handle),
rattan (shaft); length860
cm, length of handle 11
cm; 20th century

CA110　　　　P.19
兩用杖
銅、木　長90公分、杖柄
長14.5公分　20世紀
Dual-purpose cane
Copper (collar), wood;
length 90 cm, length of
handle 14.5 cm; 20th
century

CA111　　　　P.79
藤枝手杖
藤　長104公分　19世紀
Rattan cane
Rattan; length 104 cm;
19th century

CA112　　　　P.107
牛角柄竹節手杖
牛角、竹　長80公分、杖
柄長11.5公分　20世紀
**Bamboo cane with
cattle-horn handle**
Cattle-horn (handle),
bamboo (shaft); length
80 cm, length of handle
11.5 cm; 20th century

CA113　　　　P.41
海象牙柄木杖
海象牙、木　長89公分、
杖柄長11公分　20世紀
**Walrus tusk and wood
cane**
Walrus tusk, wood;
length 89 cm, length of
handle 11 cm; 20th
century

CA114　　　　P.52
竹節手杖
竹、銀環　長91公分、杖
柄長12公分　20世紀
Bamboo cane
Bamboo, silver (collar);
length 91 cm, length of
handle 12 cm; 20th
century

CA115　　　　P.73
嵌銀絲百壽杖
木　長90公分、杖柄長
10.5公分　20世紀
**Cane inlaid with one
hundred "shou"**
Wood with silver inlay;
length 90 cm, length of
handle 10.5 cm; 20th
century

C116　　　　P.41
羚羊角柄手杖
羚羊角、銀環、木　長79
公分　20世紀
**Cane with antelope
horn handle**
Antelope horn (handle),
silver (collar), wood
(shaft); length 79 cm;
20th century

CA117　　　　P.52
犀角柄直身木杖
犀角、金屬環、木　長89.5
公分　20世紀
**Wooden cane with
rhinoceros horn handle**
Rhinoceros horn
(handle), metal (collar),
wood (shaft); length 89
cm; 20th century

CA118　　　　P.84
銀帽直身杖
銀、木　長88公分　20世
紀
**Cane with silver cap
handle**
Silver, wood; length 88
cm; 20th century

CA119　　　　P.71
牙柄竹身杖
象牙、竹　長83公分　19
世紀
**Bamboo cane with ivory
handle**
Ivory (handle), bamboo
(shaft); length 83 cm;
19th century

CA120　　　　P.71
竹節手杖
竹　長88公分、杖柄長14
公分　20世紀
Bamboo cane
Bamboo; length 88 cm,
length of handle 14 cm;
20th century

CA121   P.65
漆雕人物藤杖
木 長184公分 20世紀
**Red lacquer cane
topped with female
deity carving**
Rattan; length 184 cm;
20th century

CA122   P.25
日本名家竹杖
竹 長164公分、杖柄長4
公分 20世紀
**Japanese craftsman's
bamboo cane**
Bamboo; length 164
cm, length of handle 4
cm; 20th century

CA123   P.88
雕龍木杖
黃楊木 長90公分、杖柄
長14公分 20世紀
**Boxwood cane in the
shape of a dragon**
Boxwood; length 90
cm, length of handle 14
cm; 20th century

CA124   P.75
玉手杖
墨玉 長84公分、杖柄長6
公分 約18世紀
**Jade cane with patterns
of lucky symbols**
Black jade; length 84
cm, length of handle 6
cm; 18th century

CA125   P.118
象牙杖柄
（右一）6.2×2.8公分 （右二）7.6×3.1公分 （右三）
8.2×3.5公分
（右四）11.8×4.9公分 （右五）6×5公分 （右六）3.8
×3.8公分
Ivory handles
From right to left (6.2×2.8 cm, 7.6×3.1 cm, 8.2×3.5
cm, 11.8×4.9 cm, 6×5 cm, 3.8×3.8 cm)

CA126   P.119
玉巧雕杖柄
（右一）4.5×4.5公分 （右二）4.6×6.4公分
（右三）5×5公分 （右四）7.3×4公分
（右五）5×4.5公分
Jade handles
From right to left (4.5×4.5 cm, 4.6×6.4 cm, 5×5 cm,
7.3×4 cm, 5×4.5 cm)

CA127   P.120
玉巧雕杖柄
（右一）8.5×1.8公分 （右二）10.3×6公分 （右三）
12.6×4.4公分
（右四）8.2×2.7公分
Jade handles
From right to left (8.5×1.8 cm, 10.3×6 cm, 12.6×4.4
cm, 8.2×2.7 cm)

CA128   P.117
各式杖柄
（右一）竹根杖柄 15.5×13公分
（右二）木嵌銀絲杖柄 4×4.4公分
（左上）銀鑲嵌象牙杖柄7×6公分
（左下）木雕犬首杖柄2.8×10.3公分
Handles
From right to left: Bamboo root handle- 15.5x13 cm;
Wood handle inlaid with silver thread- 4x4.4 cm; Silver
handle inlaid with ivory- 7x6 cm; Handle with dog
head carving- 2.8x10.3 cm

CA129   P.121
玉杖柄
後：（右一）4.8×3.2公分 （右二）7.8×2.5公分
　　（右三）10×2.7公分 （右四）10.3×2.5公分
　　（右五）6.6×3.3公分 （右六）5.1×2.5公分
前：（右一）3.6×2.5公分 （右二）4×3.7公分
　　（右三）5.1×3.1公分 （右四）2.8×3.6公分
　　（右五）3.6×2.5公分
Jade handles
Back- from right to left (4.8×3.2 cm, 7.8×2.5 cm, 10×
　　2.7 cm, 10.3×2.5 cm, 6.6×3.3 cm, 5.1×2.5 cm)
Front- from right to left (3.6×2.5 cm, 4×3.7 cm, 5.1×
　　3.1 cm, 2.8×3.6 cm, 3.6×2.5 cm)

CA130   P.116
鐵鎏金鷹首柄
鐵、鎏金 10×8.5公分
約16世紀
**Iron handle with gold-
leafing**
Iron, gold leaf; 10×8.5
cm; c. 16th century

國家圖書館出版品預行編目資料

揮日挑雲：王度杖具珍藏冊 ＝ Commanding the Sun and Moon: Canes from the Wellington Wang Collection ／ 黃春秀撰文；國立歷史博物館編輯委員會編輯. －－ 初版. －－ 臺北市：史博館，民97.08
　面； 公分
含索引

ISBN 978-986-01-5019-3（精裝）

1. 古器物　2. 圖錄

796.99025　　　　　　　　　　　　97014885

揮 日 挑 雲—王度杖具珍藏冊
Commanding the Sun and Moon
Canes from the Wellington Wang Collection

發 行 人	黃永川	Publisher	Huang Yung-Chuan
出 版 者	國立歷史博物館	Commissioner	National Museum of History
	臺北市10066南海路49號		49, Nan Hai Road,Taipei,Taiwan R.O.C.
	電話：886- 2- 23610270		Tel : 886-2-23610270
	傳眞：886- 2- 23610171		Fax: 886-2-23610171
	網站：www.nmh.gov.tw		http: www.nmh.gov.tw
著 作 人	王度	Copyright Owner	Wellington Wang
編 輯	國立歷史博物館編輯委員會	Editorial Committee	Editorial Committee of National Museum of History
主 編	戈思明	Chief Editor	Jeff Ge
執行編輯	溫玉珍	Executive Editor	Wen Yu-Chen
撰 文	黃春秀	Author	Huang Chun-Hsiu
內容翻譯	黃詩雅	Translator	Julie Huang
英文校稿	邱勢淙、孫素琴	Proof Reader	Mark Rawson, Jessie Wang
展場設計	郭長江	Designer	Kuo Chang-Chiang
攝 影	于志暉	Photographer	Yu Zhi-Hui
展覽顧問	嵇若昕、王行恭	Consultant	Chi Jo-Hsin, David Wang
展覽助理	王錦川、陳銘基、謝承佑、葉婷嘉	Assistant	Wang Chin-Chuan, Mickey Chen, Hsieh Chen-Yo, Tina Yeh
美術設計	關月菱	Art Design	Kuan Yueh-Ling
總 務	許志榮	Chief General Affairs	Hsu Chih-Jung
會 計	劉營珠	Chief Accountant	Liu Ying-Chu
印 製	四海電子彩色製版股份有限公司	Printing	Suhai Design and Production
出版日期	中華民國九十七年八月	Publication Date	August. 2008
版 次	初版	Edition	First Edition
定 價	新台幣800元	Price	NT$ 800
展 售 處	國立歷史博物館文化服務處	Museum Shop	Cultural Service Department of National Museum of History
	臺北市10066南海路49號		Tel: 02-23610270
	電話：02-23610270		
經 銷 處	立時文化事業有限公司	GPN	1009702043
	電話：02-23451281	ISBN	978-986-01-5019-3
	傳眞：02-23451282		
	國家書店松江門市		
	臺北市松江路209號1樓		
	電話：02-25180207		

統一編號 1009702043
國際書號 978-986-01-5019-3（精裝）
著作人：王度　著作財產權人：國立歷史博物館